also by

PETRA WILLIAMS

Flow Blue China

An Aid to Identification

(1971)

Flow Blue China II

"AMOY" By DAVENPORT, Collection of MRS. WOODROW WILSON

Photographs Courtesy of the NATIONAL TRUST for HISTORIC PRESERVATION

Petra Williams

Flow Blue China II

FOUNTAIN HOUSE EAST

Jeffersontown, Kentucky

Additional Copies of the Book May
Be Obtained from

FOUNTAIN HOUSE EAST
P.O. Box 99298
Jeffersontown, Kentucky 40299

DEDICATION AND ACKNOWLEDGMENT

TO

Marguerite Rose Weber

The study of the subject of
Flow Blue China presented in
my two books could not have
been published without her
invaluable work photographing the
patterns and her artistic talent
for assembling the material.

FOREWORD

If we were as the gods of old, dwelling in time unlimited, sure of our gifts, power and immortality, we, too, could enjoy the beauty around us and take our time in finishing the tasks set for us by others or by our own ambition. But, hubris aside, we hurry along through our alloted time, competing with real and imaginary challengers, trying to finish our work in order to earn leisure time to delight in the pleasures of our wonderful world.

Most of us make mistakes. A fortunate few have the ability to forget errors and keep on going. A lot of us need to take a hard second look at our work because, as we suspected, it requires amending and correcting.

My first book met a kind reception. I had directed it to a very special group of people, the collectors and traders in the relatively small field of Flow Blue China. I could not foresee that the publication would be as influential as it turned out to be. Many purchasers of the first book have written to me. Some have pointed out errors; others graciously have sent me pictures and descriptions of patterns that were omitted. The correspondence has been a great pleasure and I am grateful to all who wrote.

The reaction of some collecters has appalled me. I have received letters stating that the person has a piece of *real* Flow Blue, because the pattern is listed in the book. Others write in dismay, speculating that because they have a pattern that has not been included, the piece is not really Flow Blue. Inclusion or exclusion in a book is not the test of validity. For the most part, depend upon your eyes and personal research in the marks books listed in the bibliography to tell you if a piece of china qualifies as flown or not. Of course there are exceptions to this, but certainly the blurring of the cobalt on face and/or reverse side is easily discerned. Perhaps I did not make it clear enough that it was not possible to garner examples or photographs of all the patterns that must exist in the field. This still holds true. Certainly there are a great many patterns that are out of my ken and were not included in my first book and are not in this one, my second.

I do feel that many of the patterns I have seen could be classified as borderline Flow Blue and I am going to mention this in each case. Please believe me, however, the list is not fixed in a stone tablet, unchangeable and whole. I was sure that Oxford by Johnson was not really flown, but some of the dealers said it was, and I was going to call it borderline when a friend who is a dealer gave me the example photographed, and it is certainly Flow Blue. If you could see the plate in Amoy that we exhibit in our collection, you would say, absolutely, that the pattern was not a Flow Blue pattern. But you would be wrong, it is one of the oldest and usually very blurred examples of the old stoneware c. 1845. So it is with my notation of borderline designs in some categories. I may be wrong. I may have seen only a limited amount of the line; also I have come to the conclusion that sometimes the potter made the same pattern flown and sometimes not. The only way you can be fairly certain is to know your dealer or seller and make sure that the piece of china is what you want to buy.

After the first book was published, and owners could at last describe and date their wares and communicate with each other on an equal basis, the price structure changed and went higher. Collectors and dealers have questioned the prices I quoted in 1971; I had no intention of being arbitrary and, in fact, stated, "Price is a matter of supply and demand, of course, but your Flow Blue will not depreciate in value; it can only grow older and more valuable." (Page 111 in the foreword of my first book.)

It is a fact that the prices of Flow Blue have increased; is it not equally true that when you learn about a subject and acquire knowledge of the value and scarcity of your holdings you are better able to assess their value? What I am attempting to explain is that both dealers and collectors are aware now of the age of their Flow Blue pieces, the scarcity of certain patterns, and the dearth of some hollow ware pieces such as tea and coffee pots and cups that have been destroyed or damaged because of their fragile nature. It is human nature to put a premium on scarcity, and it is the collectors' urge to acquire a certain piece, or a certain amount of some particular ware that causes the price of it to go up. Some prices seem ridiculously high; there are always people who exaggerate the worth of their holdings, especially if some one else desires them, or if they believe that the market will advance. There are others who disparage even a fair price, either because of a lack of knowledge as to the real value of the object, or a lack of desire to possess it, and sometimes just to play the game of bargaining in order to make the owner back down on the price.

Millionaires and very wealthy collectors have traded in Canton and Trade china and porcelain and Historical Blue, and the prices in these fields are high because those who want to purchase will pay the tariff secure in the knowledge that unless an unforeseen debacle occurs, they can resell if necessary and either make money or come out even. Flow Blue is not that scarce, it just seems so to the eager collector with a modest purse. Although the cut-off date in my books is 1910, I have seen many patterns that were produced after that date. They are handsome and some day will qualify for antique status; it is a matter of perspective, and also of your own personal reasons for collecting. If you are a dealer, usually you must hold to the idea of selling what you buy or else sooner or later — and probably sooner — you will not be in business. The true dealers believe in turnover. Here I am speaking of the professionals who make a livelihood in the business, not the dilettantes who do not care if they ever sell. As for the collectors, they may be buying for any number of reasons. For the most part I have learned that they care deeply for the aesthetics of Flow Blue; they are charmed by the use of the blue and the delicacy or strength of the patterns. They seem to have a very personal pride in their own china and to freely admire other collections. A few are collecting for posterity, but for the most part this is a current and continuing delight and pride. Most feel a definite link with the past and the potters who made their dishes, they are for the most part nostalgic about the romance and beauty of the era portrayed in the patterns. Most of my contacts do not use the dishes, they are displayed around their homes with both skill and great pride.

A matter of interest to me is the large group of really young collectors in Flow Blue. Many are in their twenties and early thirties. They too are smitten with the blue itself and also they feel they are investing wisely in wares that they can sell if necessary when they need to do so. They look for bargains, as does every antique seeker, but they study and learn about the characteristics of Flow Blue and actually know a great deal about dating and about the potters of the past. This is because they take time to study the books that will help them in their collecting. The dealers know an old truth, they help keep each other in the business. In other words, a dealer trusts another reliable dealer, and buys from him to enhance his own stock, and the collectors should learn that if it is a matter of question as to validity and truth, it is best to go to an honest dealer.

The prices set themselves. I have been implored to make up a price list, and perhaps some day after the field settles down I will attempt to do so, but until, like water, the prices find their own level, any list would be artificial and unfair to both dealers and collectors. As a matter of fact the prices quoted in 1971 still hold true for most patterns of the later Victorian era. The oldest stoneware has been very high for years and a lot of it is now in museum collections, but there are still bargains to be found. Some of the late patterns have proved to be general favorites and many people are competing for the pieces that are difficult to obtain, therefore the prices can be very high; as I stated before, it is a matter of supply and demand, and may I add, it's a matter of what a thing is worth to the purchaser. Do not buy anything if you feel you may be cheated or if it entails a sacrifice that you may regret.

People come from all over the country to see the collection at Fountain House East. They are most welcome as long as they call or write and make an appointment. I have learned a lot from them, and their questions and comments spur me to further research. One question that has been posed is about cobalt blue and its properties. Somehow, somewhere, someone got the idea that cobalt was dangerous. Like so many strange rumors the word spread, and after I heard this from several persons, I wrote the following for the newsletter of the National Association of Dealers in Antiques. It is self explanatory and I quote it in full:

FLOW BLUE CHINA — TREASURE OR TOXIN?

In the early days of transfer printing on earthenware it was discovered that the blue used from cobalt was the only colour certain to survive the high temperatures of the glaze process. This rich, dark blue which we associate with the early historical ware and which was used for Flow Blue was prepared from cobalt oxide. This had been discovered in 1545 in Saxony by Schurer. He processed the cobalt oxide and named one of the products "zaffir", and a finer form, "smalt". This blue sank into the porous ware and then blurred a bit in the glazing period, thus giving a softness to the finished product.

"In the 1820's it was discovered that although the blue would blur naturally, it could be made to flow by instilling lime or chloride of ammonia in the sagger while glazing. This deep blurring covered printing faults and stilt marks and served to hide other defects such as glazed bubbles. Some of the pieces made are so flown that it is impossible to discern detail, and some are done so lightly that only a halo effect appears. Other colours were used to make flowing ware, such as puce, sepia, and mulberry, but blue was by far the most popular. It is of interest that cobalt was brown when applied, and the blue appeared after firing."

The above was taken directly from my book, 'Flow Blue China — An Aid to Identification,' published in September, 1971.

Since the book went to press, many people have come to Jeffersontown, Kentucky to view the collection of blue transfer patterns on exhibit at Fountain House East. On several occasions I have been told that Flow Blue is not being made any more because of the dangerous properties of cobalt. At first I scoffed and said that this was nonsense; people had eaten from plates decorated with dark blue patterns since the early 1800's. However, after six or seven different persons, wide-eyed and sincere and somewhat alarmed, repeated the same tale, I decided that some research was in order.

Cobalt is a very strong metal. It is silver-white in color and is related to nickel and iron. The word itself is German and means "underground spirit." It does not rust or tarnish and is used to plate other metals. Cobalt blue, ceruleum and smalt are used by artists in the paint and ceramic industries.

In medicine, cobalt is placed in a nuclear reactor and bombarding neutrons in the reactor cause the cobalt to emit gamma rays (like X-rays). The cobalt is **not** radio active until after this process.

A call to Celanese Chemical Division (of Jeffersontown) led to a telephone call to the Davis Company which offers a line of nine different cobalt blues, all used in the paint industry. I was advised by a spokesman for the Davis Company to call the Shepherd Chemical Company in Cincinnati which supplies most of the pigments used in ceramic painting.

According to a letter received from a spokesman of the Shepherd Company, most of the blues used today are cobalt aluminate and are approved by the FDA to be used on cans. Shepherd sells tons of cobalt for many uses including overglaze and underglaze decoration of china. As a matter of interest, the letter stated that neither smalt nor zaffir has been made for about 30 years and that there is nothing toxic about cobalt.

Therefore, let us hope that another scare rumor can be dispelled by facts. Flow Blue is **not** poisonous; and as the young mods say – 'BLUE IS BEAUTIFUL!'.

(Petra Williams, Author "Flow Blue China – An Aid to Identification".)

It is necessary to stress again that the photographs in the books are not always as fine as we could wish. Of necessity we have sometimes depended upon pictures sent by amateurs, and still feel that it is best to use them in order to give the reader at least an idea of pattern placement. We do the best written description that is possible. The rest of the pictures are made at Fountain House East. The reader must be aware that if the two books published had been done with perfect individual colour photography the price would be prohibitive. Thus, the very group of people we wish to reach would be barred from buying copies of our books. In a time of rising prices, we have sought to produce the second book at a reasonable price. Museums, libraries and schools purchased the first book for their reference rooms and we are proud that interest was manifested from these sources.

We again use the same dating methods that were used in the first book. EV again means Early Victorian, 1835 to 50s; MV will mean Mid-Victorian, 1860s-70s, and LV, Late Victorian 1880s through the early 1900s. The mark numbers will again be those used by Mr. Geoffrey Godden in his definitive work, "Encyclopedia of British Pottery and Porcelain," and I urge any serious collector to purchase this book and that of Cushion and Henry, "Handbook of Pottery and Porcelain Marks." From these books you can also learn the registry system used in England. These books are listed in the bibliography of my first book, and also in this book.

Also it is important for the reader to remember that I cannot often date a pattern exactly; therefore we will use the letter c. before the date given, and that c. stands for *circa* which means about, and in this book means within a period of a few years before or after that date.

Another question that is often raised is whether or not old flow blue patterns are being reproduced today. I have seen none, nor has anyone brought an example to my attention. There are new dishes on the market now. One has an impressive backstamp featuring the British coat of arms, and another is being made for an antique dealer in Pennsylvania, but they are backstamped. If you study the marks books, you will learn that potteries change their hallmarks every few years, and if you make use of your knowledge, you can protect yourself from mistaking a modern china article for an old collectors' item.

Dates that are printed within the pottery mark on the backstamp are not the date of the issue of the pattern. They refer to the founding dates claimed by the manufacturer, and can refer back to the very first in a long line of succeeding firms. Several plates have been offered us with the date 1790 incorporated in the backstamp. One of these is Spanish Festivities made by George Jones & Company, after 1910.

But let us return to the premise that we all make mistakes and that some of us are compelled to reconsider our work. We felt that we had to get the first book quickly into print for two reasons. I was honestly anxious about the lack of knowledge about Flow Blue, however I would have enjoyed the research, rewriting, rechecking and adding patterns and deleting errors as long as possible. Then we learned that another book was being prepared on this subject by one of our correspondents. There had been so much time and money invested in our research, photography and in collecting specimen patterns that early publication seemed only fair to those I love who were giving their time and money toward my effort.

So now you have Volume II in your hands, a continuation of the subject matter of Volume I, but with added methods of detection and study and also containing corrections and additions to Volume I. After each category, you will find a section that corrects the same category in Volume I, and also in those cases where we have located examples of the patterns described but not pictured, you will find these in the same place.

It would be real effrontery to say, "There, that's it!" All the flow blue patterns are not herein catalogued. Many more will turn up, of course. Nor is this book intended to be the final authoritative work about the subject. A pattern may be omitted because it dates after 1910 or quite simply because it has not been brought to our attention. Patterns have been included that may very well be borderline cases and may not really be Flow Blue. The collector must rely on personal good sense as well as the written word.

Many people have written and offered Historical Staffordshire pieces as examples of Flow Blue. Of course these are deeply printed with very dark cobalt, and of course they are blurred and hazy and dark, but as I stated in Volume I, this subject has been professionally documented (Volume I, Foreword) and should not be considered part of our field of study.

I am most grateful to all the dealers and collectors who wrote to me, who sent photographs, gave us examples for the collection, and did research on their own and sent me the results. They helped to fill in the blank parts of Volume I, and encouraged me to write this companion volume. Again my special thanks to Edith T. Miller who is a gracious and generous friend, and who allowed us to photograph her unique collection for use in the shapes section drawings, and helped to seek out elusive examples that we felt must exist; and I am indebted for help to Marvin and Jeanne Smith, Robert and Peggy Wright, Arthur and Elizabeth Ahrend, Judy and

Jerry Peabody, Kathryn Hoffmaster, Jeannie Peters, Phyllis Donahue and Kelvin, Kathryn Van Horn, Elizabeth Lanham, Lois Tucker, Sharon and Bobby Daugherty, Fred P. Weber, R. Fusey, Dorothy Smith, Carl and Ruth DeFranco, Harry and Paula McManus, O.C. and Martha Lam, Mary and Henry Teloh, my editor, F.W. Woolsey and my patient typist Donna Biddle.

I thank the readers who studied the first book and by their enthusiasm and letters of pleasure made it mandatory that I really try to finish my task; but most of all I lay my gratitude at the feet of Him who allowed me time on this earth, the precious gift that only He can bestow.

Jeffersontown, Ky   Petra Williams
June 1973

FOREWORD – REVISED EDITION

The first book in our study of Flow Blue China, *Flow Blue China, An Aid to Identification*, published in 1971, has been revised and republished this spring (1981). Undertaking a pioneer and continuing studious pursuit such as this calls for frequent corrections and additions to the original material. Many of these come from today's collectors who are intelligent, knowledgable and well read; they have access to much more information about antiques than was available just twenty-five years ago, and they correspond and report their findings with enthusiasm and factual proof.

We have just revised the third book, *Flow Blue China and Mulberry Ware*. Prices have advanced because of inflation, and also because of the growing interest of an informed sector of the public who want to collect, preserve and invest in part of our heritage. This has been proven astoundingly true of the collectors of Flow Blue china; therefore we have published a revised edition of this book which contains the comparative value for the Victorian items decorated by the Flow Blue transfer process. In order to keep the whole series up to date we decided also to revise *Flow Blue China II* this year (1981).

The collection of Victorian Flow Blue china which was amassed and displayed here at Fountain House East has been given to the Margaret Woodbury Strong Museum in Rochester, N.Y. When the Museum opens in 1982 the collection will be on public display.

As always, I am very grateful to all who have helped with this expanding effort to encompass the field of Flow Blue china, and, as always, I am devotedly grateful to the Creator who granted this woman the opportunity to disclose and describe a part of the history of Man's effort to create beauty in the humble field of domestic earthenware.

Jeffersontown, Ky.   Petra Williams
June 1981

CONTENTS

ILLUSTRATIONS

Cover   CARLTON by Samuel Alcock; water pitcher 12½" high.

Frontpiece   Collection of Amoy by Davenport. Pictured is the collection of Amoy that belonged to Mrs. Woodrow Wilson, the wife of the 28th President of the United States. These dishes were acquired by Mrs. William Holcomb Bolling of Virginia. (Née Ann Wigginton.) Tradition has it that she was impoverished during the Civil War, and unable to afford this set of good china, she set to work knitting socks for sale and paid the entire cost from her needle work. Her son was William S. Bolling, and when his mother died in 1899, he and his wife inherited the set of china. Edith Bolling Wilson was their child, and the dishes went to her after her mother's death. The inset photograph is a portrait of Mrs. Wilson.

The set consists of a nest of twelve platters, gravy boat, two covered butter dishes, a sauce tureen, a salad or potato bowl, two milk pitchers, a soup tureen, a covered octagonal vegetable dish, twenty-four deep soup plates, twenty-one pie plates, ten demi-tasse cups and saucers, nineteen dinner plates, eighteen supper plates, sauce bowl with cover and three serving dishes for vegetables. The set is almost complete except for the breakage inevitable in a period of use of over a hundred years.

The collection can be viewed at the Wilson's home in Washington, D.C., located at 2340 S. Street, which is now the property of the National Trust for Historic Preservation.

All examples photographed from Williams' collection except where duly noted.

A SIMPLIFIED HISTORY OF THE EVOLUTION OF THE FORMS USED IN VICTORIAN CERAMICS

The shapes of dishes and drinking containers and holloware (teapots, sugar bowls, creamers and pitchers) differ so widely in the Flow Blue field, that it has occurred to me to wonder why this should be so.

How did people first manage to eat and drink? Did primitive man find that eating a piece of cooked meat from a stick was certainly less painful than tearing it off a carcass and eating with bare hands? And then, did he figure out that he could place his portion on a large leaf as is still done in parts of India? Drinking water in your cupped hands will do, but shells were a lot more convenient and did not leak. Gourds have been found in Egyptian tombs dating back to 3500 B.C. Gourds served people without metalware or pottery; they were used for cutlery, utensils, scoops, ladles, fishnet floats, whistles and rattles.

The story of the beginnings of the art of pottery is lost in a time long before history. Perhaps pre-historic man noticed that footprints left in some clay mud, dried and retained their forms. Thus the idea of pottery may have germinated. Baskets lined with mud were probably the first water carriers. When the mud dried in the sun, it hardened sufficiently to hold its shape even after the basket was pulled away. Although fragile, these rough jars could be used for food storage.

Then, probably by accident, it was discovered that when these crude shapes were left in the fire, or when hot coals were put in the clay lined baskets to be transported to another hunting ground, the clay hardened and became sturdier. If the baskets were burned off, the exterior of the containers showed the basket weave design. In Egypt at a very early date, bowls were carved from rock, but by 3000 B.C. the Egyptians made pots. They put the clay forms in the fires with the openings toward the earth, and as a result, the inside of the finished products were black; the outside, because of elements of iron oxide rust in the clay were reddish. Since no oxygen was available on the inside, the interiors turned dark with the iron particles and smoke.

The potter's wheel had been discovered just about this time and mass distribution of clay objects commenced. Until the advent of the wheel, women who did all the household tasks, made their own pots and platters as part of their domestic duties. Jars were needed for storage of seed and grain. To carry water spherical bowls with spouts inserted were used. For the most part, these vessels were made by coiling long, spaghetti-like lengths of clay around and around in a circle starting at the bottom center, and building upward, layer by layer into the desired shape. The form was then smoothed and fired in hot coals and ashes.

Some primitives used the paddle and anvil method to make bowls. They would place broad bands of clay over a mushroom-shaped stone, then allow it to dry a bit before beating it with a paddle to make the clay smooth and firm. Bowls made by this method have been found in Polynesia. Drinking cups 8 inches high, shaped like a bell have been found in Europe and England. They are brownish and reddish and date to 2000 B.C. The people who made them are known as the Beaker Folk.

Historians believe that the potter's wheel was first used in Mesopotamia and the Near East (Turkey, Syria, etc. today) in 3250 B.C. Following is a chronological list of dates and the locales where the wheel first appeared.

2500 B.C., Troy
1800 B.C., Mainland Greece

750 B.C., South Italy
400 B.C., Upper Rhine Basin
50 B.C., South England
400 A.D., Scotland
1550 A.D., The Americas

With the wheel, it was fairly easy to make round shapes; plates, bowls, cups. These were much more symetrical than the handmade vessels. Pottery became a business and the men folk took over. In Greece many types of vases were made that can be seen in the great museums of the world. Originally the word vase meant useful pot; and vases were made for domestic use and for rituals at shrines and graves.

Cups were sometimes made of leather sewn together, and cups have been found made of pottery that imitated these even to the stitches. We will learn that pottery objects were often copies of articles made of other mediums.

Copper was being used in Egypt before 4000 B.C. and was being smelted in Crete in 3200 B.C. The Trojans were great metal workers, and obtained silver from Spain. Cups of gold and silver were found in the ruins of Troy. Also in Troy we find one of the first imitations of pottery decorated to look like silver (2000 B.C.). In Egypt, as in Crete, the art of pottery making degenerated with the advent of metal.

Silver and gold, as well as tin, copper, lead and mercury were known to the ancients, especially in Egypt, and were in use before 3500 B.C. This is because silver and gold could be used without a complex separation or refinement process, could be beaten into thin sheets, and formed into shapes. The precious metal items were reserved for royalty and the wealthiest aristocrats. Scraps of gold and bronze from the early Bronze Age (2900-2650 B.C.) have been found in the diggings in Greece. The words Bronze Age in this context did not mean a mixture of copper and tin, but was copper contaminated with gold, silver, tin and other elements which primitive metal workers could refine. But by the year 2000 B.C., the use of metal increased in Greece as a result of a technical improvement through raising the heat in the furnaces used to melt the metals. The ancient Romans ate and drank from silver services of bowls, plates and goblets. Gold was limited to the Imperial House.

Vitrified feldspathic stoneware was made in China before the seventh century A.D. and is commonly regarded as the forerunner of porcelain. Stoneware with kaolin and feldspar added are very like porcelain lacking only whiteness and translucency, and are sometimes referred to as porcellaneous stoneware (therefore the term "semiporcelain"). Stoneware made like this does not require glazing, it will vitrify in the kiln, that is, become like glass and impervious to seepage by liquids. When a glaze is desired on stoneware the glaze must withstand very high heat in order to fuse with the body. Salt glaze was the most common but this gave a pitted effect much like the skin of an orange. Later glazes made of lead and subsequently of feldspathic types were used to achieve a brilliant, smooth surface. The Chinese were able to make porcelain from the ninth century on and kept the precious secret process to themselves. During the fourteenth century the art of painting in colours on this translucent body was perfected and exquisite porcelains were competing with jade and fine metal objects as works of art.

From the days of the Romans the people of Europe were aware of the beauty of Chinese silks and traded with the far-off land, so when porcelain became available it, too, was eagerly sought. Marco Polo told of it when he described his travels in China and his seventeen years at the court of Kublai Khan (c.1275).

Christopher Columbus was seeking a trade route to India and China when he set forth to the West. Vasco da Gama, a Portugese, succeeded in reaching the China coast and by 1557 the Portugese had set up a trading post on the island of Macao. The Dutch, who were aggressive merchant seamen, were very interested in the China trade but they could not get past the Portugese, because in order to reach Canton the Chinese required that a ship stop at Macao and hire a native pilot to take the craft thirty miles up the Pearl River to Whampoa and anchor there. It was at Whampoa that cumshaw, a sort of gratuity, was paid to the representative of the Cantonese merchants who made up the Co-hong, a guild of no more than twelve merchants authorized to trade with the foreigners. The ship was left at anchor and the Captain and his commercial officer, who handled the purchasing and loading of the cargo, went with an interpreter to Canton ten miles up river. This was done in small Chinese boats or in Western cutters. When they arrived in Canton, they met with one of the Co-hong merchants who took their order and delivered previous orders that had been filled. The Co-hong merchant made the long trip to the porcelain-producing city of Ching-te Chen, but it was very worthwhile; the Cantonese merchants accrued great fortunes in the trade. The Dutch did not give up easily when they were so close to the prize; they set up a post on Formosa in 1624 and obtained tea, spices, silks and porcelains, and in 1762 they finally secured a place in Canton. The British East India Company was formed by a charter issued by Queen Elizabeth in 1600, and initially trade with India was the predominant business. However, in 1699 the company focused its interest on Canton and by 1715 it was apparent that the English were destined to become the most successful and lasting of all the foreigners in China.

A great deal of blue and white porcelain was shipped from the ports of Canton, which included Hong Kong and Amoy. The ware was made at Ching-te-Chen, a city on the left banks of the Ken river, where more than 80 percent of all the porcelain made in the Ching period was manufactured. It was 400 miles away from Canton and could only be reached by a difficult journey over mountains and along rivers. The Chinese porcelain was decorated in underglaze blue and great care was taken to obtain the correct cobalt for this purpose. This blue painting was done on green ware, that is, before firing. During the period when the British East India Company and the other countries traded at Canton, most of the decoration of the pottery was done at the city by Cantonese families, and this included the children. This was especially true of the coarse ware of greyish blue body and blue drawings that was used as ballast in the merchant ships returning to Europe.

When Americans entered the trade with China they bought a lot of this ware and were able to sell it very cheaply when they arrived at home port. Of course the Chinese could and did export beautiful fine porcelain, much of it decorated to the Western taste. This was done to order from wealthy persons in Europe, England and America. But the blue and white ware of the K'ang Hsi reign of the Ching dynasty (1662-1722) made the initial and greatest impact on the Western countries.

Most of the potters of the eighteenth century tried to imitate Chinese porcelain. France had soft paste wares and Holland developed faience, called delft ware in England. Faience or delft ware was coloured white by a glaze made of tin; this was done in order to approximate the whiteness of the Chinese product. It was decorated in blue in imitation of the prototype from Cathay.

Neither the soft paste nor the delft ware was durable; both chipped easily and cracked if the temperature of the contents changed too quickly. Holland was importing porcelain from China and was enjoying a very good business selling it all over Europe, and therefore was not too interested in developing its own porcelain. England had some potteries and the potters could make earthenware, but could not discover how to make the translucent china. Pere D'Entrecolles, a Jesuit priest stationed in China had written to Europe in 1712 that kaolin was the necessary ingredient. But the word itself was a mystery.

About this time a man named Johann Böttger, who was an alchemist, was dreaming of a way to transmute base metal into gold. He was the prisoner of the Elector of Saxony, and after failing in too many attemps to melt common metals into gold, he proposed that he try to make faience and compete with the Dutch. A factory was set up in Dresden for this purpose. He succeeded in melting the red earth of Nuremberg with a mixture of local clay and in 1708 made a "Red Porcelain" teapot very much like the famous red teapots being brought into Europe by the Portugese traders from China to supply the tea drinkers of the day. There were no potters in Dresden and workers had to be imported and were held virtual prisoners. Böttger noticed that white earth which remained white after firing was difficult to fuse and he searched for a flux with alabaster added which would act as a catalyst; his great fortune was finding a clay like kaolin and the secret of porcelain was his! In 1710 a royal patent was issued for a factory to be built overlooking the city of Meissen; at first red ware was issued and after 1713 porcelain was produced.

Böttger died in 1719. The process was kept as secret as possible but was carried from the factory by workmen who ran away from Meissen, and about the middle of the eighteenth century there were many established porcelain factories in Europe.

In 1772 the production of porcelain was started at Sevres in France. This ware was as expensive to make as to buy. A dinner service made for Queen Marie Antoinette consisted partly of plates that each took two months to make. Only the most wealthy people of the time could afford items made of Sevres china. Porcelain was made in Italy at Capa de Monte (c.1743) under the royal patronage of the King of Naples. Soft paste wares were being made in England but the glaze cracked and the body stained. Bone ash was used at the Bow factory in 1747 and this did aid against warping. In 1794 bone china was being made by Josiah Spode, II, which was composed of 50 percent bone ash, 25 percent stone. This too is a porcelain.

It is now apparent to the reader, I trust, that from the days of royalty in Egypt, Greece and Rome, to the Court of Marie Antoinette, it was the kings, queens, and court officials, and aristocracy of Europe and England who ate and drank from vessels made of precious metals, priceless porcelain and rare and expensive glass. These were all palace wares, limited to the use of those of unlimited pocketbook. From the fourteenth century and standard until the seventeenth century silver services were used on the tables of the wealthy; salt cellars, ewers, goblets and pairs of basins to wash the hands were all *de rigeur*. Plates, bowls, spoons and knives were frequently composed of silver. From 1650 silver became more common for domestic use, but the wares intended for the use of the aristocracy were made elegant by appropriate decoration.

Gold always was rare in England for economic reasons, but noblemen commissioned very large silver items such as wine cisterns and coolers. Baroque styles were popular because a maximum effect could be achieved by embossing gadroon borders, lambrequins and acanthus leaves on the vessel. But the beautiful Chinese porcelain ware was also used and cherished. In 1682 John Emely gave directions for making a salad and said that it should never be served in metal bowls, pewter or silver, because the dressing was "acetous". The proper salad bowl "must be of porcelain or of Holland delftware".

Rococo patterns followed the Baroque style and dated from the early part of the eighteenth century. These featured swirling movement and much surface ornamentation consisting of naturalistic features such as crustaceans and shells and vegetables, or romantic Chinoiserie. In 1760 a neo-classic period arose as a reaction against such fancy ware. The art of Adam predominated with its slender elongated forms and swags of laurel or drapery. Then in 1805 the Regency period saw the rebirth of the Rococo, and elaborate form and lavish decoration re-appeared. The Victorian era of our book was to see revivals of all these styles, and many others, expressed not only on precious metal or expensive porcelain, but in stoneware also.

The common herd of men, the workers, the farmers, the people laboring in the cities never even saw the great rarities that royalty took for granted. And if they had any possible access to such, they certainly had no means of obtaining such luxuries for their own use. They ate and drank from rough pottery bowls and jugs, and from cups made from leather or horn, but usually they dined and supped from treen. This is a word that describes table appliances, drinking vessels, cups and bowls made from wood from trees, therefore "treen".

The earliest specimens found are squares of sycamore wood hollowed in the middle. An oval meat platter has been found that has been incised to form a well for gravy. Stew and hash were the everyday fare of the poor and middle class, but once in a while they did enjoy a roast. At the time of Queen Elizabeth dessert dishes were being made of wood, plain on one side but decorated on the reverse with coloured arabesques and flowers. Large salt cellars were made of wood. These were double bowls with a spoon as large as a ladle. Wooden molds were made to make gingerbread, wooden coffee mills were available as were pepper castors and spice boxes. A mortar and pestle used to grind incense for a church survives. Shallow wooden bowls served nicely as drinking vessels and in the seventeenth century wassail or punch bowls were also made of wood. People ate with their fingers for the most part, but they did own wooden spoons and were expected to bring their spoon with them when asked out to dine. Forks were introduced into England from Italy in 1601. These were made of iron or steel and some for the gentry were made of silver. The first forks were long bars of silver divided at the end into two prongs. Wooden trenchers, long hollowed out logs or pieces of logs were probably the first table service. Everyone helped himself with his knife or fingers from the common trencher. *(See Notes, page 11)

The word trencher derives from the French word *tranchoir* which evolved from a word that means "to cut". In the days after the Crusades, around 1250, dinner was served before ten a.m. When the tables in a castle were set with linen table cloths and preparations were made for a feast, a silver or gold knife and spoon were set at each place, along with a neatly folded napkin. A flagon, which was a large drinking vessel, and a porringer, either of silver or gold or perhaps pewter, was placed so as to be used by two persons, usually a cavalier and a lady companion.

Also at each place there was a loaf of bread; the gentleman cut this into thick slabs and placed a slice before his lady and one at his own place directly on the tablecloth. Meat slices were served by a servant carver, and placed on the slices of bread from which they were cut into bites and eaten. The bread was not eaten; it was afterwards thrown into an alms basket for the poor, along with any scraps of meat that had not been thrown to the ever-present dogs. At great feasts silver plates might be placed under the bread trenchers for the use of the most important guests. The banquets of the day consisted for the most part of various meats such as wild boar and game and also such fowl as peacocks and swans, decorated to seem alive when served on great silver platters. This too was the time of the pastries that contained live birds that flew upwards when the pie was opened. Vegetables and fish were foods considered fit only for fast days, so most of the courses at banquets consisted of meat. It can be understood that the peasants could not waste bread to serve as plates, and so turned to the use of wood.

By the time of the Pilgrims in the new world most of the colonists ate from wood. The trencher at this time consisted of a square block of wood 10 to 12 inches long and hollowed out in the middle. When this dish became worn and rough, the block was turned upside down and the other side was made into a dish and used. These wooden dishes wore out quickly and only a few examples of early treen remain. These for the most part are in museums.

Pewter was invented by the ancients in Egypt, China and Rome. It had been in use in Europe since the twelfth century. Pewter is compounded of many variables but copper, tin, antimony and lead are its main ingredients. A strong guild controlled the making of pewter in England and since tin was readily available there, pewter was made in great quantities. The American Colonists could buy pewter objects tax free from England and did so because there was an excise tax on tin, therefore the American pewter business was slow in starting. But between 1750 and 1850 pewter became very popular and the pewterers were kept busy filling the demand for their wares, which consisted of tableware, tea pots, coffee pots, mugs, flagons and porringers. They did not fashion items for cooking because pewter is not flame proof. Iron pots were used for this purpose.

When the process of silver plating was discovered in 1850 the heyday of the pewterer was finished, as silver plate could be sold cheaply and it is tough, whereas pewter is soft and the objects made from it become mangled and damaged. When this occured the vessels were melted down and reworked, so, as in the case of treen, really old pewter is hard to find except in museums, and private collections. Also the potter's art began to supplant that of the pewter worker. With the advent of cheap pottery, the plates, tankards, saucers, mugs, and mustard pots that had been formerly made of pewter were being made of stone ware. The pewterers turned to making coffee pots as a mainstay.

Potters all over the world were seeking a medium to make dishes that would be superior to earthenware and faience and still could be sold economically. They hoped to make a product that would resemble the texture and sheen of porcelain but that would be cheap to mass produce. Earthenware was being produced cheaply, usually decorated with underglaze blue because it was safe in the kiln and small loss occurred in the potting process. According to Geoffrey Godden, 50 percent of the English earthenware produced in the first quarter of the nineteenth century was printed with underglaze blue. Porcelain which had been produced since 1757 was also at first printed in underglaze blue in order to compete with the ware from Canton, but by 1790 most pieces were overpainted with enamel colours.

Then in January 1800 John and William Turner patented a new hard china. They were the sons of the "China Man" John Turner who had a pottery and a retail shop in London. The Turners' patent was purchased by Josiah Spode in 1805 and he gave the name stone china to the ware. This new stone china looked like hard porcelain but it was opaque and was also of finer texture than the earlier earthenwares. It weighs more than earthenware and gives a clear ring when it is tapped. When porcelain was decorated with enamel the colours stayed on the surface giving a lumpy look, but on stone china the enamels sank into the glaze and presented a smooth surface which did not flake off when the dish was used. Transfer printing with cobalt was used for underprinting, in order to speed up production; and the blue design could be overpainted with enamel colours when desired. As stoneware came on the market it, too, copied the blue and white of the China Trade porcelain and the potters also copied the mold forms of the Chinese.

Coffee had been introduced into Europe from Arabia in the sixteenth century. It was very popular in London and coffee houses dotted the contemporary scene. A 1652 coffee house advertisement said coffee "quickens the spirit, and makes the heart lightsome, is good against sore eyes . . . excellent to prevent and cure the dropsy, gout and scurvy . . ." The trade flourished in England and was also popular in America in Boston, New York and Philadelphia.

Chocolate is a native of Central and South America. In 1502 Columbus took cocoa beans to Spain where the drink was made and improved upon by the addition of sugar. Spain kept the secret for about a hundred years. Then in 1657 a Frenchman opened a shop in London and sold chocolate for such a high price that only the wealthy could afford it. About 1700 the English started adding milk to the mixture and further improved its taste. In 1853 the duty was finally lowered and the drink became very popular.

Tea was imported into Europe from China around the middle of the seventeenth century. The English were great coffee drinkers and the taste for tea developed slowly. When it was first sold at Garway's Coffee House in London in 1657 it was advertised as "that excellent and by all Phitians (sic) approved China drink". Eventually it became the national drink of England.

The potters, busy making stone china and copying Chinese patterns and molds quickly turned to manufacturing the accessories necessary for this new popular pastime of taking tea. Tea was imported in small boxes of wood or silver or porcelain, which, held one and one-third pounds and were called "cattys". Thus our tea containers acquired the name of "tea caddy". Also the Chinese made small unglazed teapots of red ware and these were imported along with the tea. These pots were immediately copied by Böttger in Dresden, by the Eler Brothers in England and potters in Holland.

The Chinese made bowls for many purposes. A bowl was called a "wan", "kungwan" meant a rice bowl, "t'angwan" was a shallow bowl used for soup. A tea bowl was called "ch'a wan" and it had a cover; tea was made directly in the "ch'a wan" and in order to drink the beverage, the lid was raised slightly and one sipped through the slot, so that the leaves remained in the cup. Tea pots had been introduced during the Ming dynasty (1386-1644). Before this time vessels with spouts and handles were used for wine. But after the pots were in common use for brewing tea, bowls without handles or covers were used by the Chinese for drinking tea. These ch'a bowls were of course copied by the Staffordshire potters as they had been copied by the makers of porcelain. Tea was called "tay" in England until the middle of the eighteenth century, this was probably a corruption of the word "ch'a." Ginger jars were used in China as gift holders for tea and sweets. They were given on New Years Day with the clear understanding of all concerned that they were to be returned to be used again by the original owners. These were also copied.

9

A tea service in eighteenth century England consisted of a tea pot, a stand for the pot (a small flat tray), cups without handles, bowls for the waste tea leaves, a bowl or small basin for sugar, jugs for milk, cream and hot water, a flat sugar box with a lid, and a tea caddy. When service for one or two persons was set on a matching china tray it was called a cabaret set. Globular tea pots like the Chinese prototype were popular from 1757 to 1802; after that time china tea pots were molded into copies of silver ones and might be Baroque, Rococo, fluted or whatever. After plaster molds were perfected in 1745 porcelain potters had been able to copy the most Baroque silver tureen, with lid and tray, or any Rococo silver teapot and stand. The makers of stoneware could do this also, and because their goods were inexpensive and readily available, everyman could sit at his board and enjoy dining and drinking with a variety of dishes and serving pieces that seems bewildering to us. As styles changed from the early Baroque and naturalistic to Gothic, then to Rococo, classic and any others that filtered down from the smart set of the times, the potteries made up molds and changed designs also in order to please the public taste and meet the demand for stylish dishes.

In the Flow Blue field c. 1845, the potters who made stoneware were manufacturing the many different items that comprised the various sets of china that their customers required. We have photographed part of the author's set of Amoy, and some examples of other old patterns in order to show representative pieces. A dinner service had at least four pairs of platters ranging in size from 20 inches, with a well for gravy, down to 14 inches. Two of these had drainers that could be used under fish. Four 10-inch platters and a pair of baking dishes were in the service too. Dinner plates were 10-1/2 inches wide, soup plates were as large, and the set contained eight 9-inch plates and eight 6-inch pie plates. Also in the dinner service there was a bowl for salad and four sauce tureens with stands. Sauces were very important in a day before meat could be kept wholesome and taste buds had to be deceived with spices. Two large soup tureens with stands were in the set and ladles were made in matching pottery design for both sauce and soup.

You will, note that no cups and saucers were included. These were bought separately as a "tea set". This would include tea bowls (cups without handles) and deep saucers, coffee cups with handles, 7-inch plates, tea pot and stand, coffee pot, sugar bowls, (sucrier), tea caddy, cream and water pitchers, milk pitcher, waste bowl, two handled cake plates with molded handles and a pair of butter tubs with stands. Chocolate cups and saucers were purchased separately as was a chocolate pot. For dessert another service was required and this included fruit dishes, some oblong and some with molded handles, plates for individual servings and an elaborate center piece usually molded on a pedestal base. Cup plates were made available after the custom of taking tea was established and the cup was too hot to hold as it had no handle. Tea was poured into the saucer and sipped therefrom and the cup placed on the little receptacle designed for the purpose.

A supper set was a special item composed of four quadrant shaped dishes surrounding a central round dish with cover.

Although as time passed, pattern styles changed during the Victorian era, the types of dishes used on the table remained fairly constant. Tea cups with handles finally became the accepted fashion and handleless cups were not made to any extent after 1850. As we have learned in Book I sugar bowls became smaller after granulated sugar replaced the blue wrapped sugar cones. In the early part of the nineteenth century when tea was expensive, a large tea pot was a symbol of hospitality and largesse. Cream jugs were always rather small in comparison to the larger sugar bowls and tea pots, because cream and milk were not costly and no status was conferred by the size of the creamer.

Wedgwood had made wedge shaped and round cheese dishes since 1800 and these were also made in Flow Blue later in the century. Book I presents a comprehensive list of most of the items in Flow Blue during the Victorian age (pages 10 and 11). To this list we should add mush bowls which look like large waste bowls, and the large-handled cups, popularly called "Farmers' Cups" which were also used for mush. Honey dishes, smaller and deeper than cup plates, were used for dabs of jelly, jam and the like.

But for the most part eating customs remained fairly constant during the period in which we are interested. Dinner usually consisted of a first course of soup, which was ladled out at the table by the mistress of the house. Various relishes, including celery and other fresh tidbits were served from small dishes; cooked and raw oysters, pickles, hot fish, or sardines and soft meats such as liver and kidneys were also served as preliminaries to the main course. Bread, rolls and butter, jelly, horseradish, mustard and other condiments, including of course salt and pepper, were on the table. After the soup and *hors d'oeuvres* were removed, the main roast was brought in and placed before the master who carved it and placed the meat on heated dishes. Vegetables, other meat dishes, creamed dishes (such as eggs or vegetables), and salad were served at this time. Lastly the table was cleared and dessert was served, followed by cheese and fruit. Although most of us do not eat in such an elaborate fashion in this spartan day of diet and weight-consciousness, the format is not unlike the one we follow when we dine at a great hotel or restaurant. We might start with soup and relishes, then proceed to a main course of meat, vegetables and salad, and finish with a fancy dessert. As the French say *plus ça change, plus c'est la meme* – "the more things change, the more they remain the same."

It is interesting to speculate about the eating customs of the future. Perhaps a rainbow-coloured pill served in a floating sanitary bubble will take the place of both food and table ware and we of today shall be regarded as ridiculous primitive gluttons. Or, just maybe, on special occasions, men and women will relax and take their ease while dining together, partaking of wondrous chemical and natural foods served with grace on cherished old Flow Blue plates.

*NOTE: RE: "Shallow wooden bowls . . . ." One type known as a Mazer Bowl was used from the 13th to the 16th century. It was shallow, about 9" in diameter, sometimes had a cover, sometimes set on rounded feet, usually made of maple, trimmed with gold or silver, and decorated with an engraved or chased metal band.

RE: "Forks were introduced . . . .1601." But Norah Lofts in her book *Queens of England* (Doubleday, 1977) states that Eleanor of Castile, Queen of England, wife of Edward I, while packing her husband's goods to follow him to Scotland included on the inventory list, two forks, one of silver and one of crystal. The date was 1290.

SOME NOTES ON CHINA DECORATING
IN THE FLOW BLUE FIELD

Before transfer printing became available to potters, all china was decorated by hand. In the earliest times this was done by incising lines into the clay. The next process developed was the addition of lines on the surface by the use of thin clay, called slip, in such a way as to form a design.

By the time of the Egyptians and Greeks, artists had learned the secrets of applying colours to the vessel and could paint scenes as well as other decorative motifs. In fact the Greeks had learned how to paint on clay that was still unfired. The placing of more iron in the upper gelatin-like layer used for the decoration made this layer darker than the body and the artist could see the outlines that he was painting. Cooking vessels dating from 1056 have been found in Holland. They are small and orb shaped. Some of this pottery was decorated with slip applied by fingers in a criss-cross pattern.

After the process of glazing was discovered (the equivalent of putting a coat of glass over the baked clay during a second firing), it was possible to decorate with metallic salts on the biscuit before the glazing process. For an example copper and manganese, which fire to green and purple, respectively, could be used to paint a design which would show through the glaze after firing. These tended to blur and run as they have a low melting point and become mixed with the glaze. Then it was discovered that metal oxides obtain a better effect. But for the most part, and usually on porcelain, decoration is applied after the first glaze by the use of metal oxides mixed with a glaze that has a lower melting point than the first glaze. So if many colours were to be used, each colour was applied separately and the kiln heated to the temperature correct for that colour to fuse with the others that were placed on the ware before it. Red was last, as it required a very low kiln temperature.

Still another firing is necessary when real gold is used with an oily medium. The temperature is set so low that only the medium is burned off and the gold remains. Overglaze decoration is apt to wear away because it is not really a part of the heavy first glaze and a final glaze cannot be used as it would spoil the colours. At the time of Flow Blue manufacture we find some plates decorated in multicolours over blue cobalt. In order to fix colours over a Flow Blue background three firings are necessary. The first occurs when the clay is baked into biscuit form, the second at a very high heat sets the transfer pattern in cobalt under a glaze. If enamel is used over the glaze, a third firing is done at a comparatively low heat. Of course, if gold is used for trimming, a fourth firing is necessary. Colour was used on many early patterns, principally *rouge-de-fer* (iron red), and much later by Grindley and a few other potters of the late Victorian era.

We know the Greeks and Egyptians painted scenes on their pottery as did the ancient Chinese. We also know that floral and fauna motifs were used by the earliest potters. These were not always done in a realistic manner; frequently the flowers, leaves and animals were stylized. Border designs, used to decorate the rims and to contain central scenes were also stylized. The Greeks used a so-called 'key' design consisting of ongoing geometric squares or oblongs, and the Chinese used a similar key fret repetitive pattern.

Most indigenous pottery seems to follow the same development pattern, and we discover that early English ware was decorated with incised lines and following this, slip designs were employed. These were usually simple stylized outlines of flowers and stems or geometric motifs. When Delft ware was developed in the seventeenth century and the use of cobalt blue became general, the patterns became more sophisticated. The potters were always trying to improve the appearance of their wares as well as to making them sturdy and useful. Now they could obtain a white ground by the use of a tin glaze over the tan earthenware body, and for the first time, designs could be brush painted over the body and fired in the kiln at a heat that fused the body and the glaze.

In the eighteenth century the English potters were involved in trying to copy the Chinese imported porcelain. Since they had developed salt glazed earthenware which was fairly white, they began to paint flowers and Chinese motifs over the glaze. They used metallic oxides that fused with the glaze when placed in a muffle kiln for several hours at a low heat. ($740^o - 950^o$).

Blue underglaze transfer printing was perfected by Josiah Spode about 1781, and until 1805 most patterns were copies of those found on Chinese porcelain. Soon, however, the artists who made the designs for the copper plates began to compose designs related to western art. They drew romantic scenes of European inspiration, pictures of Gothic ruins and castles, French court scenes after the paintings of Watteau, and English country scenes.

The stylized trees and flowers of India, the Moorish details seen in Spanish lustre ware, and Japanese patterns like Imari, among many others, were all copied and freely used in borders, no matter what the central scene, and also as the main patterns when so desired. The Chinese influence remained strong just as it is today. The Willow story, discussed in detail in Book I, was a result of this inspiration. The use of the flowers found on Chinese porcelain was taken up with delight in their exoticism. To the Chinese, the Four Seasons were represented by flowers; Lotus for summer, Chrysanthemum for fall, Prunus (plums, peaches, etc.) represented winter, and the Peony, spring. These flowers and other symbols, such as the "hundred antiques", crested birds, and many more were repeated by Chinese artists with infinite variety in silk, metal, and china. The English potters copied them all and most of the earliest patterns were either copied from the Chinese or were fanciful conceptions of Indian or Chinese scenes and pastimes.

At the same time flower designs were very popular. 'Deutsche Blumen,' the flower design used at Meissen, was painted in naturalistic fashion. The famous 'Chantilly Sprigs' was brought from France by John Turner (d. 1786), who was impressed with the delicate grouping of flowers around a carnation which was executed in more conventional style than the earlier 'Deutsche Blumen.'

The earliest Flow Blue dishes exhibit all these influences. The first are hand-painted in a rather crude and simple fashion. When transfers became available Chinoiserie was the rage in all of Europe and England, and we find the English potters at Staffordshire meeting the public demand with patterns such as Oregon, Pelew, Chen-Si and Hong-Kong (1842-1845). We also find at this same time a few sophisticated florals such as "Coburg" (Dimmock), and some romantic scenes, Athens (Meigh), Rhine, Troy, and Ruins (Copeland).

As the nineteenth century progressed, style followed style, just as it does in our own time. Many European patterns became popular in England. The "Muschel" pattern from Copenhagen was well liked. This stiff floral can be seen on Haarlem (V&B). The so-called 'Onion Pattern' so routinely used on Meissen ware, was copied from the German "Zweibelmuster", which was introduced at Meissen in 1739. The word in German literally means "onion pattern", but it was a copy of a Chinese design of aster, leaves, and conventional peaches which the German artists mistook for onions.

The classical period of the early days of Queen Victoria gave us such Flow Blue patterns as 'Etruscan' and 'Theban'. We learned in the first book that the Mid Victorian era was a time of interest in many styles, and that by the end of the Queen's reign a taste revolt had set in against excessive decoration, and that the Art Nouveau movement became its spokesman.

Art Nouveau represented a real shift in perspective on design. The sentimentality of Victorian pastoral scenes, the excesses of whimsical Chinoiserie, the over-embossed, over-lustered rococo and baroque patterns now had to take a back seat to a formal stylistic approach — a linear approach, if you will — that invoked the essence of a flower or stem form. The lines still swirled, the effect was not cold, but neither was it realistic or romanticized as compared to the earlier styles. As Bevis Hillyer stated in his book, "Pottery and Porcelain," "this was the first style which set out to train the spectator for innovation."

Art Nouveau was at its height at the turn of the Century (1900). Thirty years from this writing the items made in Flow Blue with Art Nouveau patterns will pass the test of an antique, and be over a hundred years old. To the eye of the beholder of that future day, the pottery may be viewed with the same mental questions with which we view Amoy and Coburg, "I wonder who the people were who made these old dishes? I wonder who used them and who valued them? What was life really like back in those golden days? I wonder?"

THE EVOLUTION OF CUP SHAPES
ILLUSTRATED BY FLOW BLUE EXAMPLES FROM THE AUTHOR'S COLLECTION.

ABBREVIATIONS:

D – DIAMETER OR RIM
H – HANDLE
↕ – HEIGHT

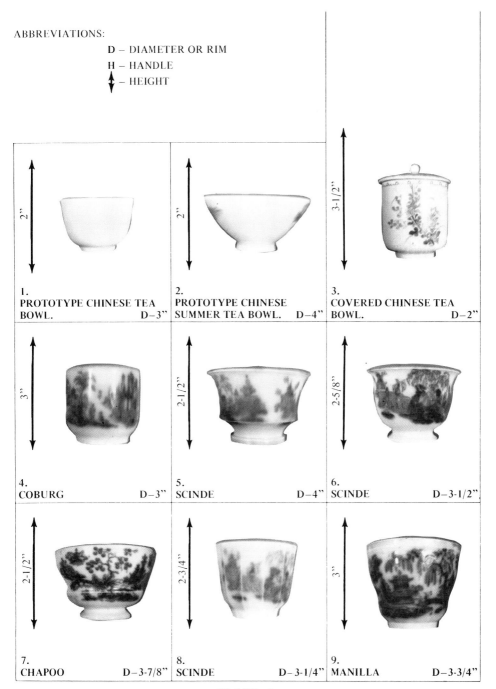

1.
PROTOTYPE CHINESE TEA
BOWL.   D–3"

2.
PROTOTYPE CHINESE
SUMMER TEA BOWL.   D–4"

3.
COVERED CHINESE TEA
BOWL.   D–2"

4.
COBURG   D–3"

5.
SCINDE   D–4"

6.
SCINDE   D–3-1/2"

7.
CHAPOO   D–3-7/8"

8.
SCINDE   D–3-1/4"

9.
MANILLA   D–3-3/4"

PLATE I

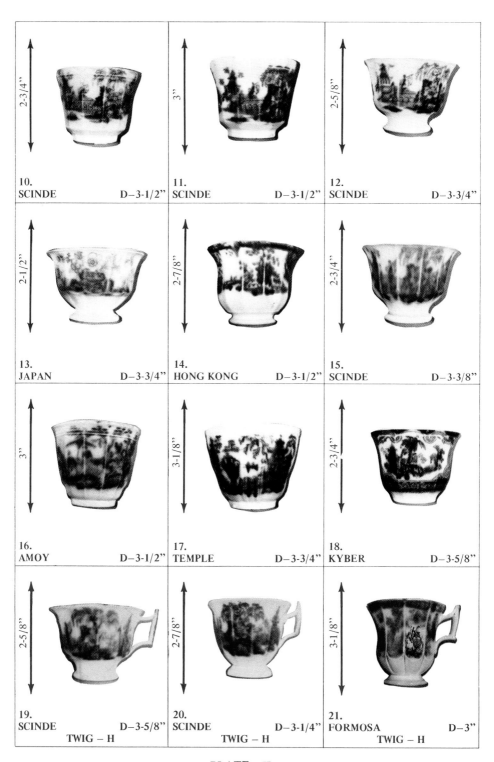

2-3/4"	3"	2-5/8"
10. SCINDE D–3-1/2"	11. SCINDE D–3-1/2"	12. SCINDE D–3-3/4"

2-1/2"	2-7/8"	2-3/4"
13. JAPAN D–3-3/4"	14. HONG KONG D–3-1/2"	15. SCINDE D–3-3/8"

3"	3-1/8"	2-3/4"
16. AMOY D–3-1/2"	17. TEMPLE D–3-3/4"	18. KYBER D–3-5/8"

2-5/8"	2-7/8"	3-1/8"
19. SCINDE D–3-5/8" TWIG – H	20. SCINDE D–3-1/4" TWIG – H	21. FORMOSA D–3" TWIG – H

PLATE   II

16

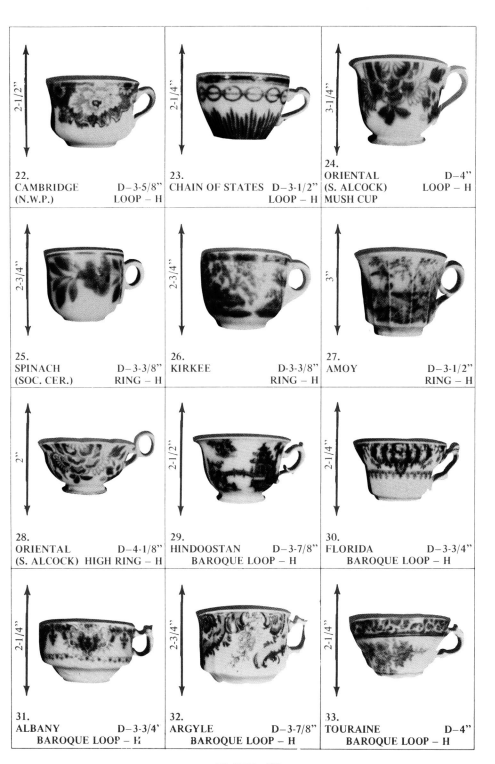

22. CAMBRIDGE D–3-5/8" (N.W.P.) LOOP – H	**23.** CHAIN OF STATES D–3-1/2" LOOP – H	**24.** ORIENTAL D–4" (S. ALCOCK) LOOP – H MUSH CUP
25. SPINACH D–3-3/8" (SOC. CER.) RING – H	**26.** KIRKEE D-3-3/8" RING – H	**27.** AMOY D-3-1/2" RING – H
28. ORIENTAL D–4-1/8" (S. ALCOCK) HIGH RING – H	**29.** HINDOOSTAN D–3-7/8" BAROQUE LOOP – H	**30.** FLORIDA D–3-3/4" BAROQUE LOOP – H
31. ALBANY D–3-3/4' BAROQUE LOOP – H	**32.** ARGYLE D–3-7/8" BAROQUE LOOP – H	**33.** TOURAINE D–4" BAROQUE LOOP – H

PLATE III

A LIST OF SOME OF THE DESCRIPTIVE POTTERY MARKS
USED BY ENGLISH POTTERS AND OFTEN FOUND
ON EXAMPLES OF FLOW BLUE

It is common in collecting china to find pieces on which there is no hall mark or backstamp, so that no pattern name or manufacturer's mark is present. However, on such pieces, quite often one can find a term such as Patent Ironstone China either impressed into the body or printed somewhere on the back. The following is a list of the nomenclature that I have found in trying to research the history of Flow Blue china. I am going to list these in calendar form, on the theory that if you memorize or at least familiarize yourself with the early qualifying names that are antiquated and colourful to our modern ear, you will easily remember the words that were used near the turn of the century. (1900).

In Volume I, I stated that creamware, developed by Josiah Wedgwood in 1761 was better looking and more servicable than stone ware; I meant to say, more servicable than the earthenware that had been developed until that date.

Potters were seeking for a medium that would be much more durable that the earthenware thus far developed, and this included Queen's Ware, and with which they could compete with the Chinese market that was sending coarse, blue painted porcelain all over the world. They needed a cross between the two products.

It is probable according to many authorities, including Geoffrey Godden that William Turner, in 1800, developed his "Turner's Patent" China, which he decorated with the oriental patterns then called "Japan" and was the first to accomplish this feat by the addition of feldspathic material, a kind of white crystalline mineral. It is assumed that he sold his Patent to Josiah Spode who started production of ware made with this method, and named "Stone China". The name was used for the hard compact bluish ware in order to suggest great strength and lasting wear. But this special new tough material that was fit for dinner and tea services because it could withstand heat was still Earthenware. Various other potters achieved good results by similar methods and about the same time, and each gave a different name to his product, hoping to sway the prospective purchaser with this form of advertising. Soon after this however, other potters copied some of the names, so in many cases you will find more than one potter listed as using the same name; for the most part they did so in the same era such as the following:

1805 STONE CHINA

Josiah Spode, printed in black 1805—1815, printed in blue 1815—1830

Davenport, impressed 1805—20 (Davenports name always present with this mark.)

Hicks, Meigh & Johnson, printed 1822—1835 (Hicks & Meigh may have used it earlier.)

John & William Ridgway, printed 1814—1830

James Edwards, printed or impressed 1842—51

Thomas Godwin, printed 1834—1854

John Maddock, printed 1842—55 (Also probably used by Maddock & Seddon, 1839—42.)

1805 NEW FAYANCE

Josiah Spode, printed 1805—33

1805 FELDSPATHIC PORCELAIN
Josiah Spode, printed 1805–33

1808 NEW STONE
Josiah Spode, impressed 1808–20 (He also used the initials "N.S." impressed.)
(Spodes name is always present with this mark).

Samuel Keeling, impressed in an octagon with SK&Co. 1840–50

1812 INDIAN STONE CHINA
Job Meigh, impressed (usually) and printed

Charles Meigh, printed and impressed 1835–49

Charles Meigh & Son, printed and impressed, 1851–61

Old Hall Earthenware Co., Ltd. impressed and painted. (This company was formerly Charles Meigh & Son and Job Meigh had used the words "Old Hall", both printed and impressed).

1813 PATENT IRONSTONE CHINA
Charles Mason patented this in July 1813. The first marks were impressed in one line or two or more, or in a circle. From 1820 the printed words appear. Mason went bankrupt in 1848.

Ridgway & Morley used it from 1842–44.

Francis Morley continued the mark and used it 1842–62.

G.L. Ashworth used it from 1862 +

1814 OPAQUE CHINA
John & Wm. Ridgway, printed, 1814–30

Ridgway & Morley, printed, 1842–44

Baggerly & Ball, printed, 1822–36

Thomas Godwin, printed, 1834–54

Mayer & Newbold, printed, 1817–33

Bridgwood & Clark, printed, c. 1857

1822 REAL STONE CHINA
Hicks, Meigh & Johnson, printed 1822–35

John Ridgway, printed, c. 1830

1824 IMPROVED STONEWARE
Dillwyn Swansea, printed, 1824–50

1828 KAOLIN WARE
Thomas Dimmock, printed, 1828–59

F. & R. Pratt & Co., printed, 1840 +

1828 STONE WARE
Thomas Dimmock, printed or impressed, 1828–59

John Ridgway, printed, 1830–55

Ridgway & Morley, printed, 1842–44

1830 **PATENT (with Royal Arms)**
    Samuel Alcock & Co., printed 1830–59

1830 **IRONSTONE CHINA**
    Hackwood, printed, 1830–40
    Edward Walley, impressed, 1845–56
    Henry Meakin, printed, 1873–76
    Alfred Meakin, printed, 1897 +
    J & G Meakin, printed, c. 1890
    G. L. Ashworth & Bros., printed, 1862 +
    W. Adams & Co., printed, 1890 +
    Wood & Son, printed, 1910

1830 **OPAQUE GRANITE CHINA**
    William Ridgway & Co., impressed 1830–54

1833 **PEARL**
    Deakin & Son, impressed, 1833–41
    Charles Challinor, printed and impressed 1892–96

1834 **IRONSTONE (in a curve & impressed)**
    Mellor, Venables & Co. 1834–51
    T. Walker, 1845–51

1834 **PEARL STONEWARE**
    Podmore Walker & Co., printed, 1834–59
    Wedgwood & Co., 1860+ (Enoch Wedgwood was actually a partner of Podmore
    Walker)

1835 **PORCELAIN OPAQUE**
    Charles Meigh, printed, 1835–49

1835 **DRESDEN IRONSTONE CHINA**
    John Meir, impressed, c. 1835

1835 **FRENCH**
    Charles Meigh, printed or impressed, 1835–49

1835 **IMPROVED STONE CHINA**
    Charles Meigh, impressed, 1835–49

1835 **REAL IRONSTONE CHINA**
    C. & W. K. Harvey, printed, 1835
    G. L. Ashworth & Bros. printed & impressed, 1862 +

1835 **ORIENTAL STONE**
    John & George Alcock, impressed, 1835–43

1837 **IRONSTONE**
    John Meir, printed, 1837–97
    John Wedge Wood, printed, 1845–60
    W. Adams & Co., printed c. 1870+

1838 PEARL WHITE
Wood & Brownfield, impressed, 1838–50
E. Walley, impressed, c. 1856

1839 INDIAN IRONSTONE
John & George Alcock, impressed, 1839–46

1839 WARRANTED STONE CHINA
Joseph Clementson, printed, 1839–64

1842 ROYAL PATENT IRONSTONE
T. & R. Boote, Ltd., printed 1842–96

1842 IMPERIAL STONE
Ridgways & Morley, printed, 1842–44

1842 IMPROVED GRANITE CHINA
Ridgway & Morley, printed, 1842–44

1845 PATENT OPAQUE CHINA
Francis Morley & Co., printed, 1845–58

1845 REAL IRON STONE
Jacob Furnival & Co., impressed, 1845–70

1845 ROYAL STONE CHINA
Francis Morley & Co., printed, 1845–58

1845 CHINESE PORCELAIN
T. J. & J. Mayer, printed, c. 1845

1846 STAFFORDSHIRE STONEWARE
Cork & Edge, printed, 1846–60

1846 PEARL WHITE IRONSTONE
Cork & Edge, printed, 1846–60

1851 OPAQUE PORCELAIN
Charles Meigh & Son, impressed & printed in a curved line, 1851–61

1853 IMPROVED OPAQUE CHINA
Impressed with EF & Co. Elmore & Forster, 1853–71

1857 PORCELAIN OPAQUE
Bridgwood & Clark, printed, 1857–64
Sampson Bridgwood & Son, printed, c. 1885
Cochran & Fleming, printed, 1900–20

1859 IMPERIAL IRONSTONE
Morley & Ashworth, printed, 1859–62

1860 WARRANTED
James Edwards, impressed in small, straight letters c. 1860

1861 **SEMI PORCELAIN**
Henry Alcock, printed, 1861–1901
Henry Alcock Pottery, printed, 1910–35

1870 **SPECIAL WHITE STONEWARE**
Clementson Bros., printed, 1870+

1870 **ROYAL PATENT STONE WARE**
Clementson Brothers, printed, c. 1870

1870 **PARISIAN GRANITE**
Sampson Bridgwood, printed, c. 1870

1875 **IMPERIAL IRONSTONE CHINA**
Cockson & Harding, printed, 1875–77
Birks Bros. & Seddon, printed, 1877–86

1880 **PORCELAINE DE TERRE**
John Edwards & Co., printed, 1880–90

1880 **WARRANTED IRONSTONE CHINA**
John Edwards & Co., printed, 1880–90

1881 **GENUINE IRONSTONE CHINA**
E. Boddely & Co., printed, 1881–98

1883 **ROYAL SEMI PORCELAIN**
T. G. & F. Booth, printed, 1883–1901
Furnival Ltd., printed, 1890–1910
Booths, printed, 1891–1901
Alfred Meakin, printed, 1891+
A. Williamson, printed, 1891+
Wood & Son, printed, 1891–1907
Johnson Bros., printed, 1900+
Ridgways, printed, 1905–12
Alfred Cooley & Co. Ltd., printed & impressed 1909–14
Sampson Bridgwood, printed, c. 1912

1893 **ROYAL IRONSTONE CHINA**
W. Baker & Co., printed, 1893
Cochranes & Fleming, printed, c. 1896+

1896 **IMPERIAL STONEWARE**
W. Adams & Co., printed, 1896+

An impressed Rosette was used by Podmore Walker & Co. 1834-1859 and also by Enoch Wedgwood who was the "& Co." in Podmore Walker & Co. He used the word Wedgwood by itself and also Wedgwood & Co.

COMMENTS ON RELATED AMERICAN MARKS

The early American potteries copied many English marks including the Royal coat of arms because English pottery was considered superior to that of all other countries.

American potters used the term "Stone China" starting about 1853 and the words "Ironstone China" appear also. Frequently the word "warranted" accompanied these terms. For example, L.B. Beerbower of New Jersey used the words "Warranted Stone China" (c. 1879). Many companies used the term "Ironstone China" plus "Warranted" on their backstamp. Among these were the Vodrey Pottery Company of East Liverpool, Ohio (c. 1896), and Knowles, Taylor & Knowles, also of East Liverpool (c. 1870). The Wheeling Pottery of Wheeling West Virginia used the words "Royal Ironstone China" above a royal coat of arms, and the word "Warranted" underneath it (c. 1880). The Mercer Pottery Company of Trenton, New Jersey used the words "Warranted Superior" over a pair of shields, and the words "Ironstone China" beneath the mark. Incidentally, this double shield mark was composed of an American flag design and an English amorial design. James Moses, an American, who organized the Mercer Company in 1868 joined with a Mr. Carr, also an American and Edward Clarke, an Englishman, to form the International Potteries. This double shield design was used by the Mercer Pottery Company, by the International Pottery Company of Trenton, New Jersey, by Burgess & Campbell, who purchased the International Pottery Company in Trenton and by Edward Clarke in Burslem, England, 1880-7. The same shapes were made at the Mercer and International potteries and the goods were interchangeable. But the English potter did not use the words "Warranted Superior" over the shield as the American companies did. Clarke used the words "Trade Mark" instead. In only one mark did Mercer do this.

The word "Warranted" appears to be a selling term used often on American backstamps and very rarely in English marks.

"AMOY" By DAVENPORT

"AMOY" By DAVENPORT

Oriental Category

ASIA
Maker Unknown

This large cup (4 inch diam. and 3¼ inch high) is not marked. This name is used to present the pattern. It is decorated with a scene that contains a lady holding a parasol, she is seated on a balcony that projects from a multi-roofed pavilion at the left of the picture. Tall willow trees flank the building and an overscaled flower is at left. The base is composed of arched rock forms. A lake is indicated by straight lines and in its center there is a boat and at right and in the background there are rock forms and a house.

In the foreground there are two little figures, one is seated and holds a sunshade, the other is standing near a pail and holds a hoe.

The border design appears on the inside rim and consists of foliated cartouches containing diagonal lines and a long geometric design over a leaf. These alternate with rectangular reserves containing a peony flanked by leaves and tendrils.

English or Dutch, probably E.V. or M.V.

ASIATIC BIRDS
Maker Unknown

This serving dish has embossed pierced scrolled handles which are white and gold. Its rim is decorated with four elongated oval reserves containing exotic flowers. These are separated by narrow bands of striated leaf forms.

The well is encircled by a key fret design. It is almost covered by a drawing of overscaled flowers, slender tall leaves, and a pair of birds with split long tail feathers. The birds face each other, the one at left is flying and the other is perched on a tall flower stalk.

There is no backstamp on the plate, the above name is used for cataloguing purposes.

Probably English, probably M.V., c 1860–65

BASKET

Maker Unknown

This is a picture of a miniature saucer. The border design is of three scroll reserves that enclose a diamond diaper pattern and which alternate with a pair of flowers separated by a large vertical 'S' Scroll.

The center picture is of a stylized round basket sitting on a scrolled platform and containing a formalized flower with leaves and tendrils.

The backstamp consists of a printed quill and the number 204.

BIRMAH

Possibly Made by Wood & Brownfield

This old plate is fourteen sided and is panelled. The edge is outlined by a double blue band that is intersected in five places by a pair of elongated and embossed leaves.

On the plate there are three large highly stylized flowers shaped like a square or a star with realistic buds and sprigs. These are placed in the well, and are separated by three small flower sprays, each different.

The name is probably meant to be "Burma".

The backstamp offers only the pattern name and the letter C. Goddard says on page 713, it is unwise to attribute the letter C.

However, this same blank was used by Wood and Brownfield (see "Ambrosia" Williams, first book) and the border and embossed leaf treatment is identical to this pattern. Since they potted at Cobridge, it is just possible that this is their work.

Probably English, marked "C", probably E.V., c 1845.

BOMBAY JAPAN
Could be Minton

This plate is unevenly scalloped and its edge is outlined in yellow lustre. A border design of scrolls is almost obliterated by a dark blue band. The rim is decorated with four evenly spaced sprays of dahlias, leaves and buds. The well is defined by a dark band that contains oval inserts.

The center design shows a vase at lower center from which overscaled sprigs of prunus rise to left and top center. Another spray is placed at the right. A small butterfly appears at top center. However, gold and purple paint have been applied heavily all over this design and it is difficult to distinguish the details.

The backstamp is an oriental urn surrounded by small flowers. On the base appears the word "No", but no number is printed. A deep "B" is impressed into the body and an artist has written 1607 in yellow. (See Ormsby, Pg. 85, Minton Mk. 8) Minton did make stoneware until 1836 according to Ormsby.

English, like mark 2695, E.V., c. 1835

BROSELE
Maker Unknown

This small coffee can-shaped cup is decorated with a stylized oriental scene of country houses, fields, trees and a lake. A small boat is in the right foreground and there is a pagoda at right rear. Gold has been placed on the trigger handle of this cup.

BURMESE

Possibly Made by W. & E. Corn

This cup is printed with a fishing scene. Two men with nets are on the bank under a large willow at the right and two other persons are approaching the bank in a boat. At left there is a large pavilion and in the center distance there are other buildings, a towered pagoda and a mountain. The printing is done in slate blue.

German   or   English   (probably), marked ⟨W⟩, *L.V., c. 1891.*

BYZANTIUM

Made by Brown, Westhead, Moore & Co.

The rim of this compote is decorated with a twisted rope design, each loop enclosing a flower form and set against a background of horizontal lines. The well is encircled with hairpin loops and tiny dots.

The center scene shows nomad tents in the foreground placed in the shade of two very tall trees. A small group of persons garbed in turkish clothes are seated on a rug in the center. In the middle ground there is a flat roofed castle with a garden at the right. Beyond that there is water on which small ships are sailing and in the distance rise minarets and domes and a wall surrounding a city, presumably Constantinople, the former name of which was Byzantium.

The mark used is the old Ridgway "belt and ribbon" mark (3269) that had been used by John Ridgway, Bates & Co., and then Bates, Brown, Westhead, Moore, and then by the above named company.

English, marked B.W.M. & Co. Mk. 676 and Mk. 3269 L.V., c. 1900.

CABUL

Made by Edward Challinor

The plate photographed is fourteen sided and panelled. The border is printed with an outer edge of a small diaper pattern contained in a dark line that is interrupted at four points by a scrolled flat cartouche form that contains a leaf design. Between these cartouches there are stylized flowers with scrolls and a pedestalled urn.

The center scene depicts at left a lady carrying a parasol over her headdress and holding a bird on her outstretched hand. She stands at the top of three steps on a little porch and a small figure stands behind her. There is a plant in a jar beside her. At the right is a very large urn on a pedestal; the usual overscaled flowers appear at ground level on a paved terrace. Behind the urn are tall ferns and a palm tree. A boat is placed on a body of water in the center distance and on the horizon there appear mountains.

English, Mk. 835A, Dated Aug. 26, 1847, E.V., c. 1847

CANTON

Made by Ashworth Bros.

This pattern has been made to look like the primitive type of Chinese pattern that was sent to the American colonies and to England as export ware from China. The border edge is criss-crossed and so is the band encircling the well.

The drawing of water, houses, islands, arched bridge, and small boats is overscaled and painted loosely on purpose to gain the effect of the early Canton Ware. There is no pattern name on the backstamp and we will use this name for cataloguing.

English, Mk. 147, L.V., c 1891

CANTON

Made by James Edwards

This pattern is very like "Pekin" by Dimmock and gives the same appearance, but the elements composing the design are different.

The border is covered with a diaper pattern of diamonds and the picket edge is formed by thick fleur-de-lis forms.

The core of the geometric design in the middle of the plate has four scroll-trimmed diamonds radiating from the center circle and four little ovals between the diamonds.

Note that the center design on the body of the pitcher has been hand painted, and extended into an oval.

Marked "Warranted" (Impressed) and as above, English E.V., c. 1845

CANTON GRUP

Maker Unknown

The edge of this plate is evenly scalloped. The rim is decorated with coiled fern fronds, stylized flowers, and dark scrolls. There are four oriental key designs equidistant on the lower part of the rim. The well is wreathed with a zig-zag brocade containing four rectangular floral medallions. A large bouquet of stylized exotic flowers and dark leaves almost covers the entire well. At top center there is a small butterfly and at right rear there is a little garden house perched on a trellis base. The pattern name is printed on the base and there is no hallmark.

Could be Dutch, probably M.V., c. 1860

CHANG

Made by C. T. Maling

This photograph is of a small bowl that is printed in slate blue. The rim is decorated with an enclosed wide band that contains cartouches formed by scrolls and filled with a diamond diaper pattern. These alternate with small scenes of a stylized temple and a landscape.

The main design depicts a large teahouse at left. A mandarin is seated at the top of a flight of stairs. A woman stands near him holding a parrot and another woman is approaching with a tea tray. At right there is a garden house and tall bamboo trees. There are other buildings in the center distance.

The second picture shows a handless cup in the same pattern. It is possible that this was made by C.T. (Christopher) Maling's father, Robert, who owned the pottery until 1859. The cup is printed in dark cobalt.

English, marked as above, Mk. 2487, made in Northumberland, L.V., c. 1880

(This pattern is the same as Ning Po made by Ralph Hall, c. 1845. See page 39, Book I)

CHINESE

Made by John Meir & Son

This cup plate is ten sided and is panelled. The rim design is composed of 8 squares of checker board alternating with horizontal trellis in which flowers are set. A thick wreath of twigs surrounds the well.

The center scene shows a garden house at the right with tall trees behind it. In the foreground are two little figures, one seated on a railing. At left across some water there is a small temple, and there are mountains in the distance.

Marked J. M. & Son, Mk. 2635, M.V., c. 1870

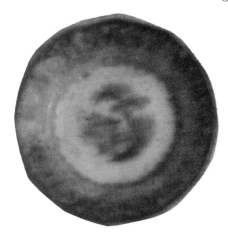

CHINESE ARABESQUE
Made by Petrus Regout

This is a fourteen sided cup plate which is panelled. The design on the rim is made of arabesque curves, the points of which invade the well and form a wreath around it.

The center design shows a many roofed pavilion at the left and a tall graceful tree at the right. In the center there is a railed platform.

Dutch, marked as above, M.V., c. 1875

CHINESE BELLS
Maker Unknown

Vertical lines of varying lengths edge the rim of this saucer and form a spear point type design.

In the center there are two small figures, one straddles a railing and the other sits on it. They are dressed in tunics, pantaloons, and large coolie hats. One is holding a long pole that has crossed pieces at the top from which bells are suspended. Stylized flowers appear at the right side of the scene and a stylized bouquet is in an urn at the left.

There is no backstamp on this dish so the above name is used to catalogue the pattern.

CHINESE DRAGON
Probably Made by F. Morley or Ashworths

The compote pictured is one of a pair. It is panelled at the top and the mold is ribbed and so is the base.

A large dragon is depicted coiling around the base and upward and around the body. The vessel is also decorated inside with a smiliar motif.

English, marked Masons Patent Ironstone China, Mk. 2530. This mark was used by Mason, then by Francis Morley, and finally by G.L. Ashworth & Bros. It can be dated pre 1862 when Ashworth added that name to the mark.

CHINESE KEY & BASKET

Made by William Brownfield & Son

The rim of this plate which was photographed at the Tallman Restoration in Wisconsin is decorated with five reserves containing different knot designs which are emblematic. These are placed on a field of Chinese key fret pattern.

The center design is contained within a ring and depicts a large oval basket with a tall handle. This is filled with stylized flowers and the handle is topped with a ribbon bowknot.

English, marked as above, Mk. 666, (variation with "Trademark"), L. V., c. 1885

CHINESE TREE

Made by Thomas Dimmock

This plate falls within the gaudy range of decoration, but the underprinting in cobalt on the plate is flown. Its outer edge is detailed with a tan border of diamond and dot diaper design interrupted in four places by dark blue leaves. The rim is printed with henna coloured flowers, cobalt leaves and stems. The well is encircled with a wide tan band of diamond and quatrefoil diapering in which are placed four floral oval medallions.

The center design covers the well and depicts a tree, the trunk of which is tan and brown, which bears iron-red flowers and blue leaves. Near the base of the pattern the flowers are overscaled and there are also some blue dahlia-like flowers in the center of the lowest part of the pattern. A butterfly is at middle right.

English, marked with an intertwined "D", also impressed Pearlware, Mk. 1300 (specific mark 1301), E.V., c. 1840

CHING

Made by Davenport

This twelve sided panelled deep dish has a border design of three reserves rimmed at the top with a floral band and at the bottom with leaves and scrolls that decorate the well. The reserves are connected by six Gothic diamond shaped shields, each containing a cross, and edged at the top with fleur-de-lis.

An overscaled bird flies at the top of the center scene which contains two persons, one of whom is seated and is fishing, while the other stands and holds a ring containing a parrot. Stylized flowers and rock forms complete the picture.

English, impressed Anchor mark, Mk. 1184, E.V., c. 1840.

CHRYSANTHEMUM

Probably Made by F & R Pratt & Co.

This honey dish is not panelled and does not have a shaped outer edge, but the edge bears a design of alternating checks and diamonds. Four cartouches on the rim, each containing a stylized flower, are linked by a field filled with geometric bird-like forms, and the design enters the well and is contained by a single gold line. This same border was used by Pratt with a different center design and on a different mold with the name 'Shusan'. The central design depicts an oriental-inspired chrysanthemum. This dish bears no name and may be a version of 'Shusan'.

English, M.V., c. 1855.

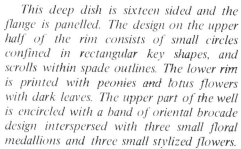

CHUSAN

Made by Francis Morley & Co.

This deep dish is sixteen sided and the flange is panelled. The design on the upper half of the rim consists of small circles confined in rectangular key shapes, and scrolls within spade outlines. The lower rim is printed with peonies and lotus flowers with dark leaves. The upper part of the well is encircled with a band of oriental brocade design interspersed with three small floral medallions and three small stylized flowers.

The central scene shows oriental furnishings; a large throne-like chair is at the center, a table with a closed oblong box and two vases is at the right rear, and a large jardiniere filled with tall flowers and plants is at the left. In the foreground there are fans, a jar topped with a dog of Fo on its lid, and an open work ceramic garden stool.

This pattern was also issued after 1862 by G. L. Ashworth (Mark 146) English, marked F. M. & Co., Mk. 2760, E. V., c. 1850

CORAL JAPAN

Probably made by Samuel Alcock & Co.

Many potters of the early Victorian era put forth versions of 'Japan' designs, which consisted for the most part of printing a design in underglaze blue and then adding enamel colours after the first glaze. Here cobalt has been used so that it flowed into the entire surface of the dish. Many colours have been added in the overpainting, pale yellow, orange, light green, rose and bright coral-red rouge-de-fer.

The design on the rim of the irregularly scalloped plate consists of three shield designs containing the diamond shaped oriental symbol for rocks; these alternate with three floral groups. The well is circled by dark blue leaves and green and red scrolls.

The central design pictures the usual exotic flowers, coupled with small flying insects.

English, marked 'Florentine China' and a printed beehive device, see Godden page 28, E.V. c. 1845

CYPRUS
Made by Davenport

The twelve-sided panelled plate shown has a line of circular scrolls around its outer edge. The rim is printed with four large peonies separated by scrolled urn-like designs.

The deep well is encircled by a band of the rounded scrolls interrupted under each of the rim designs by thicker scroll work.

The central picture is of a large temple at left; it has balconies and upturned roofs, shuttered windows, and panels of fret work. It overlooks a lake at center and at the extreme right is a tall palm tree. Behind the temple and to the left, are tall trees and a small tower.

In the center distance there are porches and a small pavilion. At the front left there are exotic leafy plants.

English, marked as above, Like Mk. 1186 (impressed mark 1181A), E.V., c. 1850

DAGGER BORDER
Made by Thomas Dimmock

Here is Dimmock issuing his version of the China Trade Canton design that was so popular at the time. The design components include mountains, pagodas, boats and arched bridges, but Dimmock added the distinguishing touch of a row of spear points on the inside of the outer criss-cross band.

We also show a picture of an old *Canton* plate. It is cruder in rendition than the Dimmock example, and the blue used is a pale greyish blue. Another version of this old pattern that can be studied is Ashworth's *"Canton"* in this book.

English, marked D, like mark 1298, E.V., c. 1844

DELHI

Made by Blackhurst & Tunnicliffe

The border on this little plate is printed with a scrolled and circular motif that alternates with a design of four curled plumes that form an M that points toward the wall. The upper well on this cup plate is encircled with four small prunus branches under the plumes.

The center design shows a cylindrical tower with cone shaped top at the right having a square geometrical design probably representing a flag projecting from its right side. At left is an overscaled flower at the base of a large symbolistic tree, surmounted by a garden house and bamboo fronds. In the center stands a small figure in pantaloons and a peaked hat. He is holding a tall staff which is topped by a triangle and three bells.

Two pictures are shown of this pattern. Miniature teapots, such as the one photographed, are fairly rare. We photograph this one in order to illustrate that sometimes the central design motif does not appear on the body of hollow ware. The border design is clear and indicates the pattern.

English, marked B & T, Mk. 401, M.V., c. 1879

DELHI

Possibly Made by W. & E. Corn

The edge of this scalloped saucer is printed in slate blue with a row of twigs. The rim design consists of three scenic cartouches. These are separated by a flower and square pattern placed at the top of a lace-like field. Both designs are united at the well by a thick wreath of tiny flowers, garlands, and fleur-de-lis

Tall palm trees are at left in the center picture and a temple with arches, onion-domed towers and minarets are at the right. In the center foreground there is a tall urn on a pedestal.

English (probably), marked , L.V. (probably), c. 1891

D'ORSAY JAPAN
Made by Minton

This deep dish is polychromed and there-fore has many colours. But deep cobalt was used on the border in the striated panels, in the leaves of the floral pattern and in the center. This blue was allowed to flow into the white surface of the dish, and the reverse side is stained very blue.

The center design is typical of the period, and shows a small table at left with a vase and incense burner placed on it. At the right there are the usual overscaled exotic flowers.

English, marked impressed as above and "BB" (Best Body) Mk. 2706 impressed date 1868, M.V. 1868.

FISHERMAN
Possibly made by Podmore, Walker & Co.

The sauce dish photographed is small (5 inches) and very shallow. It is ten sided and is panelled. The rim is dark edged and is trimmed with pairs of full blown roses that alternate with cartouches formed at the top by scrolled fleur-de-lis and contained at the bottom by garlands of small flowers.

The central scene contains a very tall tree at center, and under it, a man is fishing from a river bank. At right is a large farm house with a square tower, and at left front there is an oriental garden house with a fancy fret work railing around its porch. In the back-ground and to the left, there are other buildings and trees.

The plate is marked with an impressed rosette. There is no backstamp, so the name given here is used for cataloguing.

English, probably E.V., c. 1850

FLOYDS AMHERST JAPAN
Maker Unknown

The saucer photographed is gently scalloped. The rim is covered with a delicate tracery of small flowers and leaves, and in a few places there are dark short foliated scrolls.

The central design is composed for the most part of the same tracery, but two overscaled flowers and some large leaves are printed in dark cobalt. At left, in the background, there is a small garden house and a fence.

According to a picture in Bevis Hillyer, Page 145, (see Bibliography), Charles Floyd was an English, earthenware dealer in London in 1835. But this plate appears later than that date.

English, marked with the title and "ironstone" on an open scroll.

FONT
Made by Broadhurst & Green

The border of this saucer is printed with Indo-oriental designs of scrolls and little sprig forms.

The central scene covers the well and extends upward on the rim. There is a pagoda placed at right and a similar building appears in the center distance. There is a tall spray of water from a flower shaped basin fountain at left, and a willow tree arches high above the scene. In the foreground are the usual overscaled flowers.

Both the Green Co. and Broadhurst Co. were located at Fenton after 1870.

English, marked as above, Mark not located, L.V., pre 1891.

FORMOSA
Made by the Southwick Pottery

This vegetable dish is printed with the same border and the exact design of flowers and fence that appear on "Carlton" by Samuel Alcock & Co. (See Vol. 1, page 15, "Flow Blue China", Williams, 1971).

English, marked SB & Co., impressed Scott, Thorne pg. 71, Mk. 13 E.V., c. 1838

GEISHA
Made by Ford & Sons

The plate pictured is scalloped and embossed. The rim is decorated with scrolled cartouches separated by a tulip-shape design on a zig-zag background.

The central design covers the well. A large three tiered pagoda is at right in the middle ground. It is linked by a saddleback bridge to a rocky island at the left on which there is a tall gnarled tree. A small form with parasol is at extreme right, and there is a parapet in the foreground. The clouds above the scene are represented by heavy, wavy, horizontal lines.

English, marked F & S, Mk. 1583, L.V., 1893.

GRASSHOPPER AND FLOWERS
Made by Charles Meigh

This gaudy type plate has a cobalt transfer pattern on the rim of lotus flowers and buds. The deep well is decorated with a band outlined with gold that contains four floral reserves and four very dark reserves that contain scrolls.

The central pattern depicts a large bouquet of many different exotic flowers and at the top right a grasshopper is perched on the stamens of a striped lily.

The entire plate has been overpainted with various shades of rouge-de-fer and accented with gold.

There is no pattern name on this plate.

English, marked "French China" in an octagon E.V., c. 1842

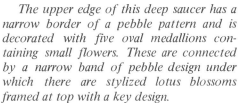

HINDOOSTAN

Made by Cockson & Harding

The upper edge of this deep saucer has a narrow border of a pebble pattern and is decorated with five oval medallions containing small flowers. These are connected by a narrow band of pebble design under which there are stylized lotus blossoms framed at top with a key design.

The central transfer depicts a pagoda in the middle, with tall palm trees beside it at the right. Further to the right a figure with a parasol stands on a platform. An extension of the platform juts into the foreground where there are overscaled flowers. A bridge runs from the pavilion to a rocky bank at left occupied by a large flowering tree. A tiny figure stands near the building at left. In the left distance there are other buildings and trees. Note that this pattern is almost identical to "Tonquin" by Carr, except for the tree detail at right center and the omission of the child's figure on the platform.

English, marked C & H, (impressed Late Hackwood), Mark 1868 exact, Mk. 978 also applies, E.V., c. 1856

HINDOSTAN

Possibly made by Wood and Brownfield

The edge of the platter photographed is faintly indented at eight spots. The border design is geometric, somewhat Moorish in feeling, with triangles enclosing stylized flowers alternating with a spearhead design on a floral field.

The center of the dish bears a drawing of the familiar overscaled exotic flowers and leaves.

English, marked W & B, Could be Mk. 4242, E.V., c. 1845

HONG

Maker Unknown

The rim of this deep saucer has sixteen panels, the outer edge is decorated with baroque scrolls from which at four points a pair of leafy branches with buds point toward the center. Alternating with these are chrysanthemums.

The central scene shows a tall flowering tree at the right front and a towered lakeside pagoda is at the left middleground. There are wind bells hung from its upturned eaves and stairs lead from its porch to the water.

In the distance there are other pavilions and towers. In the foreground at right the usual overscaled flowers are placed around some rock forms.

Could be Dutch or English, probably E.V.

HONG KONG

Made by William Ridgway, Son & Co.

The deep dish photographed is barely indented in four places on the edge, which is outlined by a band of diamond repeats interspersed with small ovals. A row of dots is placed along the inner edge. The pattern on the rim consists of three heavy scrolls surrounded by dahlias which alternate with a double diamond flanked by baroque scrolls and topped by a stylized five petalled flower. Suspended from the diamond, which represent rocks, are straight lines and a diamond-shape pendant. The well is outlined by a brocade circle of twisted rope which forms diamonds with dot centers, and this is inlaid with four oval floral medallions.

The center pattern is a stylized floral, with the usual overscaled flowers, and a willow pattern in the background. But the important element is the pair of heavy scrolls that forms the base of this design and the rim pattern.

English, marked WRS Co., and impressed "Imperial Stone", (Also The Royal Coat of Arms, marked WRS Co., is both impressed and imprinted) Mk. 3307, E.V., c. 1842

HYSON

Made by Samuel Alcock

This panelled dish has been made on a baroque mold and is unusual in that the rim is pale lemon yellow. Three large sprays of oriental flowers are placed around the rim.

The central floral design is also typically oriental and is composed of reeds, leafy branches, and tall parasol shaped flowers at left. The top flower has streamers of petals flowing from it. Gold has been painted over part of the floral designs.

The reverse of the plate is printed with three small coral-like branches and the back-stamp is a flower and leaf printed design.

English, marked S.A., impressed B, like Mk. 75, E.V., c. 1845

INDIA

Made by G. L. Ashworth & Bros.

A narrow band of tiny circles is printed around the edge of this dish. The rim is covered to three-quarters of its width by a bold design composed of many diverse oriental motifs. Four fan-shaped forms alternate with four double slanted pillar designs, and these are linked with a field of small floral and geometric figures.

The well is encircled by a band of floral and pebble forms that is inset with four floral medallions.

The center scene covers the entire well and contains trees, pavilions, stylized landscape features and several small boats, that have curved roofs, like sampans, some of which have tall poles from which large square flags are flying; these appear in the right foreground and there are other similar boats in the background.

English, marked A. Bros. and impressed Ashworths, Mks. 137 and 141, M.V., c. 1870

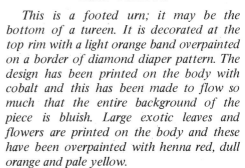

INDIAN GARDEN
Maker Unknown

This is a footed urn; it may be the bottom of a tureen. It is decorated at the top rim with a light orange band overpainted on a border of diamond diaper pattern. The design has been printed on the body with cobalt and this has been made to flow so much that the entire background of the piece is bluish. Large exotic leaves and flowers are printed on the body and these have been overpainted with henna red, dull orange and pale yellow.

Gold was added last to call attention to the openwork applied handles and the curved feet that support the vessel.

There is no mark of any kind on this tureen but the ornate molded handles and feet, coupled with the typical decoration of the period, would date it c. 1845-50. It is probably English.

INDIAN PLANT
Made by Thomas Dimmock

This wavy edged plate has a dark blue outer band, and then an inner row of scroll and fringed embossing.

The central design covers the well and consists of stylized water and rock forms. Tall plants, with slender stems and topped with long narrow leaves, probably are meant to represent hemp.

English, marked D and Kaolin Ware, Mk. 1298, E.V., c. 1844

JAPAN
Maker Unknown

Here is another example of a pattern printed under glaze in very heavy cobalt that is flown, then over painted with henna red, pale yellow, and green. The brush strokes are very distinct and the paint is wearing off, as it was applied over the glaze.

The pattern is the same as "Pekin" by Wilkinson but is condensed in order to fit the small 6-1/2" plate. (See the notes for addenda and corrections to Book I at the end of this section). This plate is marked only "Japan", which is printed in a cartouche.

English (probably), E.V., c. 1845

JAPAN PATTERN
Made by Davenport

This old dish is decorated with the typical "Japan" pattern of the period. The blue is slightly blurred and forms a halo effect around the smaller dark twigs on the border. This may be one of the forerunner patterns where the blue flowed slightly.

The plate is edged with printed beading. The rim pattern has large dark triangular reserves with white circles. These are separated by stylized buds and sprays. The well is outlined by a simple line.

The central picture is of stylized bamboo on the left, overscaled flowers at the right, and a heavy bone-shaped design at the bottom.

Marked Davenport, Longport, Staffordshire, Stone China, this name has been used to catalog the pattern as the backstamp bears no pattern name. This was usual at this period.

English, like Mk. 1182, E.V., c. 1820

JAPAN PATTERN
Made by J. & G. Meakin

This saucer is unevenly scalloped and its gilded edge is outlined with embossing of tiny scrolls and horizontal lines with palmetto fans and fleur-de-lis pendants printed with cobalt. The pattern on the rim is composed of three groups of stylized oriental flowers and leaves surrounding three different oriental objects, a pair of scrolls, a drum, and two crossed cornucopias. The well is outlined by embossed dots and a printed circle of spear point design.

The central motif is a stylized bouquet set in a flat decorative basin which is placed upon a pedestal composed of four large dark leaves.

English, marked as above, Mk. 2601, (without the Coat of Arms), L.V., c. 1891

KAOLIN
Made by Podmore & Walker

This old plate is twelve sided and panelled and the rim is decorated with six large double scrolled designs that form triangular cartouches. These alternate with a smaller scroll pattern. The well is surrounded by a spear point design.

The center scene is dominated by a large stylized flower in the right foreground. Behind it appears an arched gazebo and tall bamboo trees. A bridge crosses a lake in the middleground and leads to a small building at the left rear.

Kaolin is the name of a basic clay material found in China in the province of Kiangnan. It derived its European name as the result of an error by Pere d'Entrecolles, who in 1712, while living in China, wrote to Europe that this substance, which he called Kaolin after Mt. Kaoling in Jao Chou Province, was the important element in the process of making porcelain.

English, marked as above, Mk. 3075, E.V., c. 1850

LANDSCAPE

Made by W. T. Copeland & Sons Ltd.

This square serving dish, printed in slate blue is gently scalloped and its outer edge is decorated with a band of triangular diaper patterns. This design connects eight matching pairs of large pointed leaves that flank a small blossom, under these and part of the design there are fleur-de-lis and an oval pendant flanked by trailing stems.

The top of the well carries a deep inner border that forms arches, this consists of stylized lotus blossoms placed against a background of curved snail design.

The center scene is lightly drawn and shows a pagoda on an island at left and a house, trees, rocks, water and a garden at right.

English, marked Spode Copeland, like Mk. 1077, L.V., c. 1891

LEEN

Possibly made by Petrus Regout

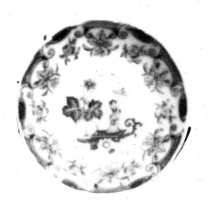

This saucer is gently scalloped and is panelled. The edge is outlined by dark cobalt ovals and arches with scrolls. The rim is covered with stylized leaves in the arches that alternate with small prunus blossoms.

The center design is composed of a table-like platform, which is in essence a cart, with wheels made of daisies, and a scroll handle. There is a large rounded jug at the left containing an overscaled flower with two leaves and a sprig. A small feminine figure stands at the right on the cart near the handles. She wears a vest and full skirt, a large headdress, and carries a parasol.

Probably Dutch, marked "R" in a cartouche, E.V. (probably), c. 1850

MACAO
Made by Davenport

This plate is slightly scalloped. The upper part of the rim is decorated with five rounded triangular reserves, each containing one-half of a stylized flower and these are joined by a scroll design. Floral sprigs of peonies and prunus are placed between these. The well is outlined by a band of small ovals.

The central pattern shows the usual pattern of overscaled flowers and leaves at the left center, and a less important vertical spray of small flowers is placed at the left. The latter is based on a scroll form.

English, impressed anchor, Mk. 1181, E.V., c. 1845

MADRAS
Made by Samuel Alcock & Co.

This is a photograph of the bottom of a covered vegetable dish. It is scalloped and the handles are gilded, embossed leafy scrolls. The rim is decorated· with trailing stems and flowers that form a continuous wreath.

The center design springs from a base of symbols for rocks. At the left there is a stalk of fern like leaves, in the center there is a trio of small oval buds, and at the right a tall flowering tree arches up and over the center.

English, marked S.A. & Co., mark 75, E.V., c. 1845

MANDARIN
Made by Thomas Dimmock

The border on this small octagonal platter has oval reserves at the corners and mid-length in which there are stylized dahlias and a fan shaped leaf. These are placed between foliated reserves containing a diaper pattern of abstract leafy shapes.

The central scene is framed by wave-like scroll reserves and small stylized flowers and stems. In the center of the picture a male servant stands on a platform. He holds a pennant and is pointing toward a seated personage who wears a royal hat. In front of them, on the ground, there is a man feeding two large fowl.

English, marked D and Kaolin ware, Like mark 1298, E.V., c. 1844

MANDARIN
Made by John Maddock

This fourteen sided dish is panelled on the rim which is decorated with large sprays of stylized oriental flowers. The deep well pictures a group of people: a man with a parasol who stands with a woman, and a pigtailed boy. At right there is a tall stylized tree under which there sits a musician playing a flute and at left rear there is a willow tree. The entire scene is circled with a wreath of fleur-de-lis.

English, impressed with a Castle mark, marked Maddock Ironstone China, Mk. 2461, E.V., c. 1850

MIKADO
Made by Thomas Furnival & Sons

This gently scalloped plate has a rim design consisting of three flowers alternating with three angular cartouches, separated by a border of different Japanese-inspired diaper patterns.

The central scene is framed by a band of brocade and a few small curving branches of cherry blossoms. It depicts the roof of a temple at the right, part of its porch can be seen and a fence is placed in front of it. At left there is a grove of tall slender pine trees.

English, marked as above, like mk. 14, page 53 in Thorne, L.V., c. 1881

MOGUL

Maker Unknown

This twelve sided plate is panelled. The rim design consists of five large cartouches that contain a single open flower. These alternate with open scrolled arch spaces containing sprawling prunus flowers and leaves. The bottom part of both designs descend the sides of the dish on the side of the well.

The center design shows a tall round tower at the right middleground. It is surrounded by water and a small boat is afloat at left; in the far center distance are other small buildings. At left an arched bridge leads to a turreted castle. Large exotic flowers and leaves form a wreath around the scene.

The back of the plate shows triple stilt marks and it is probably E.V., 1850.

NANKIN

Made by Cauldon Ltd.

The pattern on this small stand for a sauce boat has a border design composed of flowers and dark leaves. The dish is deeply scalloped and the handles are embossed with gilded leaves. On each side at the handles there is part of an unfurled oriental rolled scroll. The well is encircled by a double ring and small curved beads.

The central scene has a tall bamboo tree at the left center, a flowering bush of large flowers is placed around it. At its base there are monolithic stone shapes and two large flowers. At the right there is a small garden house on a base that is arched over the water.

English, see Kovel Page 248, Mk. M, L.V., c. 1891

NANKIN

Possibly Made by T. Walker
or Mellor Venables & Co.

This pattern is very similar to "Pekin" by Dimmock, page 43 Williams, Book 1, and appears identical to Canton by Edwards, page 14. It consists of a very dark edging band, in this case, on a plate that has a rim divided into six panels. A spearpoint edge is placed on the inside of the border. The well is outlined by another dark circle that contains four oval reserves containing calligraphy.

The central medallion is large, spear edged, and consists of a wide dark circle around a white center in which a geometric motif has been placed.

Walker used the curved ironstone mark that is impressed into this plate and he was contemporary with Dimmock and Edwards. So did Mellor Venables & Company and at the same time, so until a completely marked specimen appears, it is only safe to date the pattern.

English, marked Ironstone impressed in a half circle, E.V., c. 1845

ORIENTAL

Made by Thomas Dimmock

There are ten panels around the rim of this plate, which is printed in multicolour. The rim is printed with scrolls and chrysanthemums at four places. The well is outlined by a lattice band, interspersed with four floral ovals. A circle of fleur-de-lis borders this on the inner side toward the well.

In the center is a spray of three chrysanthemums with very dark leaves and some small prunus flowers at the base.

English, impressed "Pearlware", Printed "Stoneware" with "D", Mk. 1300, c. 1845

ORIENTAL

Probably Made by Josiah Spode

The top of the panelled sugar bowl photographed is decorated with oval scrolled cartouches containing a small flower.

The picture on the side shown features an arched bridge topped with a small building with double curved roofs. At the left of the bridge there is a pavilion flanked by tall bamboo trees. At left in the foreground there are the usual overscaled flowers and leaves.

The reverse side shows a large flower tree with overscaled leaves and blossoms. At the right top there is a butterfly and at left a bird with long split tail feathers is perched on a branch of the tree.

English, marked impressed N.S., E.V., c. 1820

ORIENTAL GARDEN

Maker Unknown

The unusual rim treatment on this plate is distinctive. The edge is unevenly scalloped and at each of the six smaller scallops a pair of matched scrolls is depicted which form a rams horn pattern. The rest of the rim is covered with a fluted pattern of dark and light blues. The well is defined by a wreath of heart shapes.

The central scene is equal to the rim design. The entire well is covered with a picture of a tower complete with spire situated on flowering rock forms. In the left foreground a mandarin and woman converse while two servants stand nearby. One holds a parasol over the couple. A tall willow tree is at left and an equally tall flower tree appears at right.

This plate has no pattern name and no backstamp. We will use the above name for cataloguing.

PAGODA

Made by Powell, Bishop & Stonier

This plate is shaped as an octagon. The straight edges are enhanced by a 1/2" band of a lozenge pattern. The rim is decorated at four points with a lotus blossom with buds and leaves. These are separated by a leaf design. All of these elements enter the well.

The central design is encircled by a narrow band of diamond design. It pictures a towered building at left from which floats a pair of pennants. A big flowering tree is at the right. These two elements are linked by a bamboo bridge. Two small figures appear on the bridge, one is carrying a pole. There is a tall tree at center left and in the distance there are a lake, a boat, and another tall pagoda.

English, marked P. B. & S., Mk. 3137, M.V., c. 1878

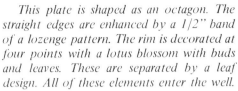

PAGODA

Made by Thomas Till & Son

This tureen lid is bordered with a band of oval medallions each containing a little scene taken from the main design, and separated by a fish scale diaper pattern. These are bound on the inner side by a row of scallops.

The central design shows an overscaled floral tree on one side of the dish and a pagoda with balcony and an arched bridge on the other. A small boat is placed near one of the handles and a flower form at the other. All these elements are very stylized, but the unique part of the design is a series of straight stemmed spear shaped leaves that appear in both of the larger designs.

English, marked as above, Reg. #65508, Mk. 3858 L.V. c. 1891

PEKIN
Made by Davenport

This plate is gently and unevenly scalloped. Five floral sprays are placed around the rim. The well is encircled with a gothic trefoil picket design and so is the outer edge on some examples.

The central pattern is a stylized floral in the oriental manner and consists of a ruffled peony, dark forms that denote rocks, and small flowers and sprays.

We show the second plate in order to illustrate how different elements were used by the same potter in the same pattern. The second plate has four rim sprays and a different floral grouping in the center.

English, marked as above, Mk. 1181A (dated), E.V., c. 1844

PEKIN
Made by Wood & Brownfield

Pictured here is the inside of a footed compote. Its outer rim has a band of diamond trellis, edged with a tiny scalloped line. Four horizontal arrangements of chrysanthemums are placed around the border. The well is encircled by a band of the diamond trellis pattern interrupted in four places by oval medallions containing a formalized flower flanked by dark scrolls. This well band is edged with the same small scallop line as on the upper border.

The central design is the usual Chinese inspired floral group of overscaled dahlias, a flat flower with leaves and a very dark lily-form rising from the grass on sinuous and heavy tree-like stems.

The backstamp has the pattern name set in a wreath of scrolls and flowers.

English, marked W. & B., "Pearl White", Mk. 4243, E.V., c. 1845

PEKIN

Made by Wood & Sons

Here is fairly late flow blue version of the Willow Story. The family house is at the right set under an apple tree. A bridge with three figures on it is in the middle, the little garden house is on an island at left, and the two birds, representing the souls of the lovers fly above the scene.

The border pattern consists of a double row of petal crosses.

English, marked as above, Mk. 4285, L.V., c. 1907

PEKING

Maker Unknown

This fourteen-sided panelled plate has an oriental key design on its outer edge. A gothic-type border design, composed of very dark enclosures that contain scrolls, alternates with oriental scenes of two little houses flanked by peonies. The well is encircled by the key design.

The central scene shows a large two-story pavilion with a flowering tree at left that is connected by a bridge to a small island at the right, which carries a walled enclosure, a tall tree, and a garden house. Two figures stand on the bridge, the taller holds a parasol.

This dish is registry dated for December 4, 1845. English, E.V., c. 1845

PERSIAN BIRD

Made by Davenport

This picture shows a platter with a scalloped border that carries a thick design of foliated scrolls. The well is encircled by spear-shaped triangular designs.

The central pattern depicts two large crested cranes. One is wading at the right and one is flying away toward the top center. At left appear the usual overscaled exotic flowers and leaves.

The backstamp also has the picture of the same wading bird.

English, marked as above, Impressed Davenport, Mk. 1887, E.V., c. 1850.

PLEASURE GARDEN

Maker Unknown

This oddly shaped dish is the top of a section of an old supper set that consisted of four such covered dishes, called quadrants, that surrounded a round covered center bowl. These sets were also called sandwich sets and were being made and sold about 1815.

This cover has an oriental lions head as a knob in the top of the cover. At the right, on the cover, there is depicted a large pillared garden house with domed roof and paved tiled terrace. At left, and toward the rear, there is another open gazebo with a round roof, in which there are three people; a little dog is standing beside them. In the center there is a stream on which a man is poling a raft. Stylized oriental trees and shrubs complete the scene.

The border design shows the man on the raft, the garden house, a village of small houses against some mountains (which also appear on the cover but are hidden by the knob) and a large flowering tree.

The lid is untitled, the base does not match (see Willow, maker unknown). This name is given to the pattern in order to catalogue.

English probably, E.V., c. 1845.

QUAN TUNG

Maker Unknown

This little deep tray is octagonal. Flowers are placed at the corners of the rim and an Asiatic bird perching on a flower is placed on the sides.

The central design covers the well and shows an exotic crested bird which is seated on a branch that contains large overscaled chrysanthemums, buds and leaves. The "Feng", or crested pheasant such as this, was the emblem of the Chinese Empress in the Ch'ing Period.

English, marked F & W, and the Name, (See Mark 4435, Godden Appendix Pg. 717), M.V., c. 1850-60.

SABRAON

Maker Unknown

The saucer photographed is printed in dark blue and ferous red. The border design consists of fish scales, cloud forms, lotus blossoms, and large leaves. These have all been over painted with dots of gold.

The center scene is dominated by large flowers and two table-like forms. In the center of this there is an open scroll illustrated with a sampan and an oriental gate-form, like a Japanese torii, and tall mountains.

The pattern name on the back of this plate is in a "Garter Mark", English (probably), E.V. (probably), c. 1845.

SCIAO

Made by Edge Malkin & Co.

Pictured is a club shaped vase with a small neck. The lower third of its body is covered with a large diamond diaper design, which is contained at the base by interlocking floral garlands and at the top by a gold band. This design is repeated at the top of the vase.

The central scene is printed in a very faded blue and is difficult to discern. There is a two storied pavilion at the left; it is situated on a lake. At the right there is a flight of stairs leading down to the water. Three figures are standing on the steps. A tall tree is placed at the right middle distance.

English, marked E.M. & Co., Mk. 1445, L.V., c. 1885

SHUSAN
Made by F. & R. Pratt & Co.

The plate photographed provides a clear example of the Chinese seal mark that this company used. It is also marked with the initials of the firm and the addition of the "& Co." which the firm used from 1840-60. As the twelve sided plate has the old triple stilt marks the pattern probably dates early in the period mentioned.

The rim design consists of six oval reserves each containing a stylized flower and leaves. These are separated by a horizontal design of the same spear pointed stylized leaves. The outer edge is bordered with a narrow band of differing oriental diaper patterns.

The design in the center of the well is composed of large stylized lilies or lotus blossoms, two sprigs of pairs of flowers, and at the right a rounded flat basket that contains two flowers and some leaves.

The tea pot is shown in order to illustrate the fact that it is important to recognize border patterns. The design of spear point leaves forms a wide band around the lower part of the body, and it is used to form a narrow wreath around the lid. But the flower sprigs placed on the upper part of the pot would not suffice to ascertain the pattern and this pot is unmarked.

English, marked F. & R. P & Co., Mark 3144, M.V., c. 1855.

SIAM
Made by Beech & Hancock

A band of small triangles edges this pattern. The rim is decorated with sprawling designs of peonies and some prunus.

The well is defined by a band of scrolls contained within narrow double lines. The central stylized floral pattern is of the usual exotic flowers of the East and vertical sprays of tall bamboo have been placed in the center of the design behind a large peony.

English, marked B. & H., with a swan, Mk. 313, M.V., c. 1870.

SINGA

Made by Cork, Edge & Malkin

This two handled mug has a different scene on each side. The first shows a lake with pagodas in the middle distance, a little boat at left, some tall trees, and a pair of deer. In the foreground, next to a tall vase, a man stands beside a seated woman who holds a butterfly-shaped lute; he is pointing to the garden house at right.

The reverse pictures a lake with pagodas in the background that are linked with a tall arched bridge. In the foreground two little figures are placed on a platform, one holds a parasol, and the other is seated and holds a long pipe.

The border design appears inside the rim of the vessel and is composed of oblong trellis cartouches that are linked with scrolls and little floral sprigs.

English, marked C. E. & M., Mk. 1101, M. V., c. 1865

TEMPLE

Made by Wood & Brownfield

This deep saucer has an oriental border pattern of scrolls and straight hooked lines that form the Chinese key design. The rim is printed in three places with a scene of a pagoda, overscaled flowers and leaves. These are separated by a fan-like design.

The center scene shows a tall open-towered structure at left. There is a fence and a tall flowering tree behind the building. At right front there are a pair of the usual overscaled flowers and buds.

English, marked W. & B., Mk. 4242, E.V., c. 1845

TONQUIN

Made by John Carr & Sons

This deep dish is unevenly scalloped. Its outer rim is decorated with a band of pebble design. Oval cartouches containing stylized floral forms are separated by geometric scrolls and stylized lotus blossoms.

The center scene covers the well and climbs the sides of the dish and shows a large pagoda in the center. At right and front of the building there are porches. On the right porch a man and child are standing. The man carries a parasol. At far right is a two masted boat. At left a bridge links the pagoda to a flowered bank and there is a figure standing on the bridge near the pagoda. A tall stylized tree with circular flowers towers above the scene at center right.

Note that this pattern is almost identical to "Hindoostan" by C. & H. except for the tree and child detail.

English, marked as above, Like Mk. 778, M.V., c. 1861.

TONQUIN

Made by Clementson & Young

The tea pot photographed has a border around the top side of the collar of diamond diaper pattern contained within scrolls that are punctuated with stylized lotus. Set between the lotus blossoms are small scenes of a pagoda with upturned roofs. A fence is at right and rock arches are at left and in the foreground.

A band of diamond diapering and oval floral medallions is placed around the upper body of the vessel and presumably around the well of plates in this pattern.

The main scene shows a woman on the balcony of a large pavilion; she is letting down a basket or perhaps a fish trap. There are two large buildings at left that are separated by a tall willow tree, steps, rock arches, and two panels of fencing. Two boats appear in the background.

The spout is decorated with a bouquet and a butterfly.

English, marked as above, Mk. 911, E.V., c. 1845

TYCOON

Made by William Brownsfield & Son

This photograph shows the top of a compote. The Japanese design consists of a pair of fans, two butterflies, an insect, and three persimmons with leaves.

The word tycoon means a person of great power and wealth, and was used in Japan to denote the shogun, the chief military commander, and the virtual ruler of the kingdom.

English, marked as above, Mk. 666, L.V., c. 1871

VASE A' LA CHINOISE

Maker Unknown

The vase photographed is about 7 inches high. Its base and collar are trimmed with a light blue band overpainted with lines of henna red. This is encircled by a cobalt scallop edged in gold. The design of flowers around the neck are enclosed with the same band.

This design, on both the neck and body, was placed on the vessel with a transfer print, which portrays peonies with leaves, branches and leafy sprigs. This cobalt flown blue design has been over painted with many colours, red, green, rose and orange. Gold has been added as the last touch to further embellish the details.

VINTAGE
Made by Petrus Regout

This photograph shows a small sauce dish, its border covered with design of three groups of stylized flowers that alternate with three baroque scroll forms that contain treillage.

In the central scene a man is walking toward the left. Over his shoulder he carries a pole from which a basket is suspended. A child stands in front of him. At left there are tall willow tree forms, and the usual over-scaled flowers. In the distance there is a tower and another building.

Dutch, marked P. R. Maastricht, M.V., c. 1860

WILLOW
Probably made by Ashworth Bros.

This unevenly scalloped plate is decorated with many colours. Iron red surrounds the edge and there is also a wreath of dark blue scrolls. The blue transfer design covers the entire-plate and consists of many elements of the willow story, the pair of doves, the garden house, the bridge and boat. A pale lime green and peach were also used in this illustration.

This pattern was first introduced by Charles and James Mason, later issued by Ashworth Bros. with the pattern name, Yin.

English, marked as above, Mk. 146, M.V., c. 1862

WILLOW
Made by Keeling & Co.

The familiar pattern of willow trees, apple trees, pagodas, and a bridge with a man crossing over it, appear on this little picture. The rococo handle and scalloped top edge are touched with gold.

English, marked K. & Co., Late Mayers, Mk. 2243, L.V., c. 1886

WILLOW
Maker Unknown

Here is the bottom of a covered dish that formed part of a supper set. (See Pleasure Garden).

This familiar scene is the typical Willow design, complete with a large house set in a garden of many different stylized trees, a zig-zag fence, an arched bridge with three figures crossing to an island, and a pair of doves, (representing the souls of the deceased lovers) hovering above. At left there is another island and a boat is on the water nearby. The border is composed of various oriental diaper designs, keys and circles.

This same pattern was used by Doulton (see Willow, Williams Book 1), but this dish is much earlier than the one photographed that was marked Doulton. Doulton was founded in 1882. This dish could have been made by Thomas Pinder of Burslem 1849-51, whose pottery became Pinder, Bourne & Hope. In 1862 the name was changed to Pinder, Bourne & Co., which was purchased by Doultons in 1878, but did not change name until 1882.

Probably English, probably E.V., c. 1845.

YEDO

Made by Ashworth & Bros. Ltd.

The rim of this plate is printed in four places with a design of dahlias with leaves and buds. The well is covered by a drawing of a zig-zag fence at left that advances to the center front. Its base is composed of heavy curling scrolls. Behind this fence at left is a lotus and a flat pad-like leaf. At right rear is placed a large overscaled dahlia with striped leaves and a tall stemmed bud.

English, marked A. Bros., Impressed Ashworth, Mk. 141, M.V., c. 1870

YELLOW RIVER

Maker Unknown

Octagon shapes like the one used for this platter were popular throughout the Victorian period. The rim of the dish is decorated with scrolled oval cartouches linked by a four-petalled stylized flower that is almost gothic in design as it resembles a quatrefoil.

A two storied house with upturned tiled roofs is set among some trees at the right of the center. A willow tree is placed in the foreground. Across a river-like body of water there are pointed mountains, some low hills indicated by stylized lines and pine tree outlines.

There is no mark on tne back, this name is used to present the pattern.

NO PICTURES AVAILABLE

BURMESE

Made by Francis J. Emery

This pattern was noted in a column. The design consists of birds, trees, branches and an overscaled key design.

English, marked as above, L.V., c. 1891

DELHI

Maker Unknown

This pattern looks exactly like "Lahore" by Corn. See Williams "Flow Blue China" Page 35, Book I.

RIO

Made by Ynysmedw Pottery

This pattern is identical to Kyber by Meir (later Adams).

It is marked Williams, and Ironstone.

Welch, marked as noted, E.V., c. 1855 (See Godden "Masons Patent Ironstone China" Pg. 114)

SINGAN

Made by Thomas Goodfellow

A pagoda appears in the right center of the well. There is a bridge to the left and a man is carrying a trailing banner on the left side of the bridge. A weeping willow is placed at the left and a pagoda is in the left distance.

English, marked as above, Mk. 1738, E.V., c. 1840.

ORIENTAL CATEGORY
ADDENDA AND CORRECTIONS TO BOOK ONE

page 13 **"BEAUTIES OF CHINA"** *Note that the central picture differs on the various pieces of a set, but the border remains the same.*

page 14 **"CANTON"** *This pattern was made by John Maddock. The mark is impressed. The maker was English, the mark is no. 2461 and the pattern dates M.V., c 1850-55*

page 15 **"CASHMERE"** *This pattern was first made by Ridgway and Morley, was marked R & M under a large Coat of Arms, both printed and impressed. The mark is 3276, c. 1842-44. It was then made by Francis Morley until 1858; next Morley and Ashworth c. 1859-62; and last by G.L. Ashworth. (after 1862).*

page 16 **"CELESTE"** *This pattern was first made by John Alcock in Cobridge, England, the print was bright blue; the mark is 67, and the date c 1855. Note that the urn pictured in this oriental scene has swan handles and bears a drawing of Grecian (!) robed figures.*

page 18 **"CHINESE"** *(by Dimmock). This pattern was also printed in cobalt without the addition of other colours.*

page 21 **"CHUSAN"** *(by Wedgwood). This pattern was issued by the same firm bearing th backstamp title "Oriental". We present a picture of a covered vegetable dish s marked.*

page 24 **"FAIRY VILLAS"** *Was first made by John Maddock and Seddon 1839-42, then by John Maddock 1842-55. For exact mark see no. 2460.*

page 26 **"GEISHA"** *This pattern is shown on a gently scalloped plate, labeled on the back "The Court Shape". It is embossed with a comb tooth design. The rim is decorated with three reserves, enclosed in foliated scrolls and urns, each contains a picture of a seated geisha, holding her mirror and accompanied by a standing attendant. These reserves are separated by a pebble design. Printed scrolls outline the rim and the well i defined by a row of trefoils placed under the pebble pattern. The central scene show the same seated geisha, but in the foreground there is a tall gowned personage, who holds a parasol and who is accompanied by a child. Registry mark should read #354458.*

age 27 **"HINDUSTAN"** *meant land of the Hindus; it is now called India.*

age 28 **"HONC"** *Should read "the well is defined by a ring of blue bands and five small scroll designs".*

age 29 **"INDIAN"** *A plate has been found that shows the entire Chinese seal mark and it is definitely not the seal mark used by Cauldon Potteries Ltd.*
But note that Cauldon did reissue Pratt's designs and could have changed the mark slightly.

age 30 **"INDIAN STONE"** *The vegetable dish shown depicts the central design of urn and flowers, and also the rim band that descends into the well. This band appears on the rim of plates in this pattern and is composed mainly of large and small flowers combined with very dark leaves. The outer edge is encircled by a diamond diaper pattern and half of a large stylized flower.*

ge 34 **"KYBER"** *This pattern, under the name of "RIO" was made by Ynsonedw in Swansea Walse. The proprietor's name was Williams and this name is included in the backstamp. (c 1850-59).*
This pattern is pictured in Mr. G. Godden's book "Masons Patent Ironstone China", page 115, plate 141.

ge 37 **"MALTESE"** *We show a better picture of the platter*

page 39 **"NING PO"** *Ningpo (sic) was one of the Treaty Ports of China that was opened in th early 1840s. The others were Hong Kong, Shanghai, Amoy and Foochow. Before th and from 1720, merchant ships had to trade at Canton with licensed merchants of th Co-Hong who were so authorized by the Emperor K'ang Hsi.*

page 40 **"ORIENTAL"** *by Alcock. After careful examination it has been decided that the pla was printed entirely in blue under the glaze, and the iron red was painted over th glaze. The red is wearing at places and the under blue can be discerned.*

page 41 **"ORIENTAL"** *by Regout. This example should be classed as borderline.*

page 42 **"PAGODA"** *The index on page 216 read that Pesank is on page 58. It can be found c page 42 as it is one and the same pattern as Pagoda. It was omitted by error fro listing on page 58 under heading "no pictures".*

page 42 **"PA JONG"** *This example should be classified as borderline.*

page 44 **"PEKIN"** *A pattern very similar to this can be seen on page 180 of G. Godden Illustrated Encyclopedia of British Pottery and Porcelain. A plate is shown ar attributed to Hilditch & Son c 1822-30.*

page 46 **"ROCK"** *According to G. Godden in his book on Masons' Patent Ironstone Chir "Rock and Rose a la Chinoise" was a pattern name of the Mason firm.*

This picture of a large basin shows clearly the Rose and the geometric double diamor figure that was the Chinese symbol of a rock.

Page 47 **"SCINDE"** *We show a photograph of the backstamp of a platter from the author's collection. A telephone call to the Historical research department of the New York Public Library elicited the information that Thompson (Jacob) & Parish Crockery was in business at 79 Pearl Street in New York in 1845-46. There is no listing for the firm after 1851.*

Page 49 **"SHANGHAI"** *by Adams. The wrong design is pictured. The small plate herein photographed is the correct example, it is somewhat blurred, but the tall tower in the center is a good distinguishing mark for the pattern, as is the towering tree at the left.*

Page 49 **"SHANGHAI"** ⟨W⟩ *mark. These pictures are reversed. Here is correct picture.*

page 50 **"SHAPOO"** *This pattern was also made by T & R Boote (mk 437) c. 1842*

page 50 **"SIMLA"** *This city is 170 miles north of Delhi and used to be the summer capital of India 1864-1947.*

page 53 **"TIMOR"** *An example was found in Sept. 1971 marked Luneville France. It is pictured here. It is printed in flow blue and colours have been superimposed on the pattern details. In February 1973 a sauce dish was acquired with the Maastricht mark that is also printed in flow blue with colours added over the glaze. In both examples lustre had been applied under the glaze and had turned a bronze colour.*

page 55 **"TONQUIN"** *by Heath. We show a clearer picture.*

age 56 **"WHAMPOA"** *The plate photographed is Whampoa and was made by The Cambrian Pottery at Swansea in Wales. The border is identical to that made earlier by Mellor and Venables, perhaps as early as 1835, and so is the central scene with the exception that the high-prowed boat and the island at the top right have been omitted. This plate bears a printed cartouche mark that reads "Improved Stone Ware Dillwyn & Co.", and an impressed semi-circular mark with "Dillwyn" over "Swansea". The bottom of the plate shows triple stilt marks, so the plate probably dates c. 1850. The Cambrian Pottery imitated Staffordshire Wares. See Ormsby page 130, mark 6. Welch, marked as above. E.V., c. 1845-50.*

age 58 **"CALCUTTA"** *No flow blue example has yet been located, this example is in sepia. The plate is twleve sided and panelled. The rim is printed with five reserves that picture a small boat and pillared buildings, and tall trees. These scrolled cartouches are separated by roses placed on a field of horizontal lines. The entire rim design is bordered with heavy scrolls that form a wreath around the well. The central picture is of a river, presumably the Ganges. There are tall minaret towers and temples on one bank and equally tall palm trees on the right. The picture is presented so that if an example is found in flow blue, the pattern will be recognized. The backstamp has the name Calcutta in an Indian design and the makers name under that (Mk. 835a).*

page 58 **"CHAING"** *This pattern has been located in many polychrome versions. (The on pictured is marked THE CHINESE PATTERN). Edge Malkin made the pattern with the name "CHANG". Hulme and Christie called it "The Chinese Pattern"; W. Adam used the name "Chinese Ching"; B & F backstamped it "Canton", and Liddie Elliot used a number- #16210. To date no plain flow blue has been located but the Adam "Chinese Ching" is printed on a pale blue that has been deliberately flown and th backstamps are dark slate blue which flowed into the surrounding area.*

page 58 **"COREA"** *This pattern is undoubtedly the one made by J. Clementson and th reported butterfly mark was a mistaken view of his Phoenix mark. This pitcher. printed in sepia; its collar is covered with a design of large chrysanthemums and leave Under this is a border of circles, scrolls and little flowers. This edging is reverse around the pedestal base.*

The central scene shows tall buildings at the left, they have upturned roofs, and at built upon a very high stonework foundation. There are two little figures at the righ One is seated and the other stands nearby. In the center of the scene there is a lake c a wide river and towered buildings appear in the far distance. At the extreme right ver tall trees arch towards the center.

ge 58 **"KREMLIN"** *The outer edge of the plates are bordered with a dark row of cobalt printed with lighter scrolls. This is succeeded by a row of linen fold scalloped draper that is fringed. The rest of the rim is printed, in this case, with a light grass green on which small white flowers have been enameled. The pattern was also sold in plain dark blue with gold accents.*

The well is encircled by a wreath of small circular scrolls contained within a single gold line.

The center scene shows a woman and small child standing at left near some rock forms and a large flowering tree. A bearded man in mandarin robes is seated at right. There is a large fringed parasol suspended on a tree branch over the man's head; a pennant flies from the top of the sun shade and a bird is perched on the right edge of it.

The honey dish shown contains a different center scene. A woman stands at left center, she is holding a basket from which two ribbons fall. At right there are some stylized rock and plant forms.

English, Marked S.A. & Co. Registry date June 14, 1843 E.V., c. 1843

PLATE VI

Reading from left to right: Sauce tureen with tray and ladle (Meigh) 6-7/8 inch by 3-1/4 inch by 4-5/8 inch high; Pedestal dessert dish (Chusan by Maddock) 8-3/4 inch diameter by 2-3/4 inch high; Fruit bowl, centerpiece (Pekin) 10-1/4 inch diameter by 5-3/4 inch high; Sauce tureen with ladle and tray (Pattern Unknown) 6-5/8 inch wide by 5-3/8 inch high; In the foreground two sauce boats, both (Fairy Villas).

Reading from left to right: Chop plate or stand for tureen (Amoy) 13 inch diameter; Soup ladle (Amoy) 10-3/4 inch long, diameter of bowl 3-7/8 inch; Soup tureen with lid (Amoy) 11-3/4 inch diameter by 9-1/2 inch high; Well and Tree platter (Amoy) 21 inch by 16 inch; Deep dish (Amoy) 10-1/2 inch diameter; Pickle dish (Scinde) 8-3/4 inch long by 5 inch wide; Deep dish (Amoy) 9-1/2 inch diameter.

PLATE VII

Reading from left to right: Sauce tureen, (Arabesque) 6-7/8 inch by 4-3/4 inch by 6 inch high; Dessert plate (Nankin by Pratt) 10-3/4 inch, including the handle by 9 inch wide; Sucrier (Whampoa) 5-1/8 inch diameter, (with handles 6-1/2 inch wide) by 4-1/2 inch high; Stand for tureen (Oriental made by S. Alcock) 14-1/2 inch by 11-7/8 inch; Syrup jug, (Manilla) 4-1/4 inch diameter, (at the widest point) by 5-1/4 inch high; Cup, child's (Fairy Villas) 3-1/4 inch diameter by 2 inch high; Sauce tureen, (Meigh) 6-7/8 inch by 4-3/4 inch by 6 inch high; Cup,child's (Delhi) 2-3/4 inch diameter by 2 inch high; Covered tureen with lid (Oriental by S. Alcock) 15-1/2 inch by 9 inch by 8 inch high.

Reading from left to right: Salad bowl (Shell) 12 inch diameter; Plates (Amoy) 10-1/2 inch, 9 inch, 8 inch and six inch; Platter (Amoy) 17-1/2 inch by 13-1/2 inch.

PLATE VIII

Reading from left to right: Round covered vegetable dish (Madras by Samuel Alcock) 11-3/4 inch long by 10-3/8 inch wide by 6-3/8 inch high; Octagonal covered dish (Indian Stone) 9-3/4 inch by 7-1/2 inch high to top of cover; Baroque covered dish (Oregon), oval 12-1/2 inch by 9-3/4 inch by 6-3/4 inch high; Octagon covered vegetable dish (Oregon) (in foreground) 8-5/8 inch diameter by 6 inch high; Covered dish, Baroque (Scinde) 11-3/4 inch by 9-1/8 inch by 6-3/4 inch high.

Reading from left to right: Vegetable dish (Amoy) 10-3/4 inch x 8-1/4 inch; Vegetable Tureen with lid (#4) (Amoy) 10-1/2 inch by 10 inch; Egg platter (Amoy) 11 inch by 8-1/4 inch; Stand for Vegetable tureen (Amoy) 13-1/4 inch by 10 inch; Octagonal platter with rounded corners (Amoy) 16-1/8 inch by 13 inch; Water pitcher, (Amoy) 2 quarts 8-3/8 inch wide (including the handle) by 10 inch high; Vegetable dish (Amoy) 10-1/2 inch by 7-5/8 inch.

PLATE IX

Reading from left to right: Saucers (3) (Amoy) 6-1/2 inch, 6 inch, 6-7/8 inch diameter; Coffee cup (Amoy) 3-7/8 inch diameter by 3-1/8 inch high; Cake plate (Heron) 7 inch in diameter (Amoy) 3-3/4 inch diameter by 2-7/8 inch high; Waste bowl (Amoy) 5-1/2 inch wide by 4-1/4 inch high; Coffee pot (Amoy) 9-7/8 inch high x 10-1/2 inch wide; Cup with twig handle (Amoy) 3-3/4 inch diameter by 2-3/4 inch high; Milk pitcher, 1 quart (Amoy) 6-7/8 inch wide by 6-1/4 inch high; Sugar Bowl with lid (Amoy) 6-1/2 inch wide by 7-1/4 inch high; Cup with round trigger handle (Amoy) 3-1/2 inch diameter by 3 inch high; Cup plate (Amoy) 4-1/4 inch in diameter; Teapot (Amoy) 9 inch high, 10 inch wide including handle and spout; Tea bowl (Amoy) 3-3/4 inch diameter x 2-7/8 inch high; Creamer (Amoy) 5 inch wide x 5-3/4 inch high.

Reading from left to right: Sauce Tureen with lid (Amoy) 7-1/2 inch x 5 inch x 5-1/2 inch; Platter (Amoy) 15-1/2 inch x 12 inch; Honey dish, (Tonguin) 4 inch; Platter (Amoy) 14-1/2 inch x 10-1/4 inch; Sauce Dish (Amoy) 5 inch; Octagonal covered dish with lid (Amoy) 10 inch; 2-1/2 quart pitcher (Amoy) 8 inch high and 9 inch wide including handles.

PLATE X

Cashmere by Morley, Collection of Mr. & Mrs. Fred Buck, New Jersey.

Scenic Category

BIRDS AT FOUNTAIN

Made by Villeroy & Boch

The outer edges of these plates have pierced borders of vertical bars. The rim itself is composed of basket weave.

The first picture shows a pair of exotic birds with crested heads in a garden setting. They are perched on the rim of a fountain that is shaped like a morning glory from which a tall jet of water rises into the air and falls back in a narrow curve. One bird with wings outstretched is drinking and the other looks upwards.

The center picture differs on the plates, and the second photograph manifests this fact with a picture of a large bird, wings outstretched who is on the branch of a tree in a sylvan setting. The correct title is INDIA. See COCKATOO, this book, page 240.

German, marked V&B, L.V., c. 1880

BOSPHORUS

Made by J. Marshall & Co.

The soup plate photographed is slightly scalloped and the rim is slightly panelled. The outer edge is decorated with a design of triangles and an inner printed row of beading. The rim is covered with a floral design of large lilies and roses with dark leaves, and some smaller flowers on a soft dark blue background. Part of the design enters the deep well and forms an irregular wreath.

The transfer picture in the center shows domed mosque-like buildings and a tall minaret (tower) at the left. In the distance are peaked mountains. Tall trees rise at the right and in the foreground on a tiered platform there are two figures costumed in Turkish pantaloons and turbans. There is a curved wall and tall post behind them. In mid-center is pictured the waterway, the strait that is called the Bosphorus, that connects the Black Sea to the sea of Marmara.

Scottish, marked as above, Like Mk. 2509, L.V., c. 1870

BROOKLYN

Possibly made by Skinner & Walker

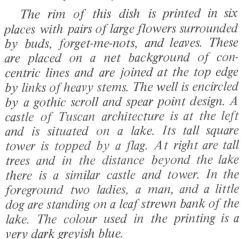

The rim of this dish is printed in six places with pairs of large flowers surrounded by buds, forget-me-nots, and leaves. These are placed on a net background of concentric lines and are joined at the top edge by links of heavy stems. The well is encircled by a gothic scroll and spear point design. A castle of Tuscan architecture is at the left and is situated on a lake. Its tall square tower is topped by a flag. At right are tall trees and in the distance beyond the lake there is a similar castle and tower. In the foreground two ladies, a man, and a little dog are standing on a leaf strewn bank of the lake. The colour used in the printing is a very dark greyish blue.

English (probably), marked Pearl Ware on a belt, Laidacker says this could be Wedgwood, M.V., c. 1870.

BRUNSWICK EVANGELINE

Made by Wood & Sons

This plate was photographed at an antique show. It is labeled "Brunswick" and has the exact border described in Book I, page 90. But in this case the well is outlined by a wreath of leaves, and in the center there is a portrait of a young woman dressed in the costume of the mid-eighteenth century. Under the picture is a line from the poem "Evangeline" by Longfellow "away to the northward Blomidon Rose".

On the reverse side a section of the poem is written across the foot rim.

English, marked as above, Mk. 4285, L.V., c. 1891.

CALIFORNIA
Made by Podmore Walker & Co.

This twelve sided plate has a border of horizontal lines. Superimposed over these is a gothic design of five circles enclosing roses and cartouche forms that contain a scene of a towered large house and its grounds.

The well is defined by a heavy circle composed of triple rows of dotted webbing.

The center scene has nothing to do with the American state of California, but is a romantic European moonlit scene of a colonnaded castle-like building, a lake and tall trees. Several small pleasure boats are placed in the lake. In the distance are high mountain peaks. In the foreground at right there is a stone parapet surmounted at the end with a tall robed statue.

E glish, Dated April 2, 1849, marked Wed.,vood, Mk. 3080 is exact mark, E.V., c. 1849

CHASE, THE
Made by Doulton & Co.

The rims of these plates are printed with bunches of grapes, leaves and arabesque scrolls, contained within narrow circular gold bands at the outer edge and at the well. The rim background colour is deep cobalt. The well is further defined by a row of egg shaped printed beading.

The center scene differs on the dishes; one shows a lady riding side saddle at full gallop; her hunting dog races beside her. The other plate bears a picture of a man, also riding at a fast pace, who is pointing the way of the game they seek.

There is no pattern name on these examples, this name is used to present the pattern.

English, marked as Royal Doulton, both printed and impressed, Mk. 1351, L.V., c. 1910.

CLEOPATRA

Maker Unknown

The edge of this plate is divided into four long scallops and is outlined by a very dark blue band. The rim is printed with five foliated cartouches containing melon-like fruits or figs. These are separated by scrolled reserves containing a large open dahlia-like flower. The bottom of both designs enter the well.

The center scene shows an obelisk and columned ruins at the left. A small pyramid in the center is almost obscured by an overscaled flower placed in the foreground. Tall flowering branches rise from this and curve towards the center. A small balustrade at left foreground is partially covered by the floral pattern.

English (probably), M.V., c. 1860

CLYTIE

Made by Wedgwood & Co., Ltd.

This platter is scalloped and is trimmed with beaded embossing. The rim is covered with a floral design, and the center picture shows a male turkey with his fan tail spread out. (Note that this company is not Josiah Wedgwood; it was formerly Podmore, Walker & Co.).

English, marked as above, Mk. 4060, L.V., c. 1908.

COUNTRY PASTURES

Made by Arthur Wood

The maker of this teapot made some other types of earthenware, but his principal product was tea pots. This example is decorated at the top scalloped, and beaded rim with dark cobalt and gold, and so is the handle. The pattern differs on each side. The transfer picture shown is a pastoral scene with horses grazing, and on the reverse side (not shown) cows are pictured in a bucolic setting.

English, marked A.W. and an 'L', Mk. 4233, L.V., c. 1910

COUNTRY SCENES
Maker Unknown

The bowl photographed is unevenly scalloped and its edge is detailed with scroll and shield embossing. The rim is decorated with large flowers, leaves and sprigs superimposed on a blue background on the upper half and over a white background below.

The center scene is of a country roadside church with a bonnet roof over its porch, and a tall steeple. There are trees and walls on either side of the road and two adults and a child are standing in front of the church steps.

English, L.V., c. 1891

COWS
Made by Wedgwood & Co., Ltd.

Antique dealers call this pattern by the above name although there is no name on the backstamp. Slate blue ink has been used for the transfer printing. The rim design contains blue oval reserves in which there is pictured a pastoral scene with two cows. These cartouches alternate with a design of large leaves on either side of a foliated oval in which there is a floral shield and a curved oval that forms an artichoke pattern.

The central scene depicts a herd of cows meandering on a stony path in a setting of low hills.

English, marked as above, Mk. 4059, L.V., c. 1906

DARDANELLES
Maker Unknown

This scenic plate was designed to hang on a wall. It is scalloped, fluted, and the dark floral edge is covered with gold lustre. The rim design consists of five small reserves, each containing a Turkish architectural scene. These are separated by large naturalistic flowers.

The middle of the well is decorated with a picture of romantic domed temples and minarets and tall feathery trees. In the foreground a man is punting a scimitar shaped boat with a gondola type roof.

There is no backstamp on this plate. The above name is used in order to catalogue the pattern.

English (probably), L.V., c. 1885

EGLINGTON TOURNAMENT
Made by Doulton & Co.

A large milk pitcher is shown here, and the name above is written in large letters across the inside of the pouring lip. The collar and base are covered with a strip of laurel leaves that form a wreath. The base also bears a vertical design of loops.

The sides show scenes of a skirmish between two knights in full armor, and on horseback, who are rushing towards each other with spears pointed at their human target.

A letter received from the Doulton Company explains that the title of the Earl of Eglington has been held by the Scottish family of Montgomery since 1508. The sixth Earl who was famous was called "Greysteel" and the thirteenth Earl, Archibald William, is remembered for the tournament that took place at Eglington Castle. This is described in the novel "Endymion" written by Disraeli.

English, marked as above (Royal Doulton) Mk. 1333, L.V., c. 1905

89

FISH PLATE II
Made by Cauldon Ltd.

The plate photographed is unevenly scal-loped. The rim design consists of a wreath of flat scallop shells and sea weed.

The central picture depicts a large fish leaping high over rocks and above rushing water.

English, marked as above, Mk. 821, L.V., c. 1900

GAMEBIRDS
Made by Wm. Adams & Co.

There are six reserves in a tassel and diamond diaper field on the rim of this plate. The diaper pattern is finished off at the well with the tassels and gives a spear-point effect. In each of the reserves there is a picture of a small game bird perched either on a stump or standing on the ground.

The center scene shows a pair of wild large turkeys. They are placed in a high mountain and lake landscape, with tall pine trees in the background.

English, marked as above, like Mk. 30, but with an eagle, L.V., c. 1891.

HACKWOOD'S GARLAND

Made by William Hackwood & Son

There is no title name on this cup and saucer. The central scene shows a woman seated on the edge of a stone wall, a man stands beside her. They are dressed in the fashion of the Fench Empire. Behind them and beyond a lake, there is a castle, and at left in the distance there are some squat towers and a very tall tree. Trees at right complete the circular picture.

The edge of the rim is outlined by a band of vertical bars, and from six points that are accented with large flowers and scrolls, deep garlands of small flowers and sprigs surround the well.

English, marked H.W. & S., and also impressed "Hackwood", Like mark 1868, E.V., c. 1846

HOMESTEAD

Maker Unknown

The scene on this cup depicts a two-storied farm house at the left. At right there is a tall elm tree and at its base is a paling fence. There is a lake in the center, and hills, trees and a barn. In the foreground are several fat sheep.

We show two pictures in order to illustrate the border design of three rows of sprigs, two rows of a Greek Key, and a top edging of spear point.

There is no name on the cup; we use this name to present the pattern.

Probably English.

ISOLA BELLA

Made by Davenport

This plate is slightly scalloped and its outer edge is trimmed with a narrow border of ivy leaves.

The central scene covers the dish and depicts a large castle at the right, mountains in the distance, and flowers and trees in the foreground.

This is a matching plate to LAS PALMAS CANARIA.

English, marked as above, Like Mk. 1194, M.V., c. 1870

ISTHMIAN GAMES

Made by Doulton & Co.

The pitcher shown has a collar printed with swags of fruit, edged at the top with a row of small gothic arch forms, and at the bottom with a white line banded in blue.

A scene of a chariot race between three chariots is pictured on the body of the vessel. Each chariot is drawn by three horses, and a boy is seen standing and holding the reins of two teams of horses. The riders are in place in their carts.

At the bottom of the pitcher there is a design of wide flat crosses centered with an oval medallion, and these are linked by small groups of fruit.

English, marked as above, Mk. 1332, L.V. c. 1900.

ITALIAN URN

Possibly made by John Ridgway & Co.

This plate is scalloped and the border is printed with pairs of realistic flowers and sprigs which alternate with a scrolled arch design that contains a stylized flower and leaves.

The central picture is the usual romantic version of European buildings placed beyond the view of a lake. In the foreground at left there is a tall romanesque urn with sculpted figures supported above three seated cupids. Behind this there are a parapet, a tall basin with acanthus leaves support, and tall trees. In the right foreground there is a small urn on a low pedestal and some roses are placed on the ground around it. There is no pattern name or hallmark on this plate. The only mark is the belt and crown. This could be a Cauldon reissue.

English, marked Iron Stone China, like mark 3257, E.V., c. 1840.

LAKE

Made by G.L. Ashworth & Bros.

The rim pattern on this unevenly scalloped plate consists of five cartouches containing two small rounded fruit forms, these alternate with five reserves containing forget-me-nots. Both are joined by long foliated scrolls placed over a background of horizontal lines. The well is encircled by a wreath of small printed scallops.

The central picture differs on the various items produced in this pattern. On this plate there is a tall tree at left, and other trees and a meadow in the foreground. In the center middle distance there is a boat afloat on a body of water. A high arched bridge, with slanting approaches, crosses over the water. Clouds and trees in the background complete the circular scene.

English, marked impressed Ashworth, Mk. 137, M.V., c. 1865

LAS PALMAS CANARIA
Made by Davenport

This plate is slightly scalloped and the edge is decorated with a narrow border of ivy leaves.

The scene covers the entire dish and depicts the landscape and palm trees of the beautiful Spanish inland called Grand Canary. The fine scenery and warm climate make this a popular resort.

English, marked as above, like Mk. 1194, M.C., c. 1870

LEIPSIC
Made by Joseph Clementson

The squat pitcher in the photograph has a thick collar band decorated with a top edging of criss-cross and diamonds, and composed of large morning glories, leaves, tendrils, and tiny flowerlets.

The scene on the body is composed of gothic church-like towered structures at right center. A dark stone arched bridge leads right from this. At far right, in the distance there are other buildings and towers. Leipsig is a city in Saxony, East Germany. Until World Warr II it was the center of German book and music publishing.

English, marked J. Clementson (with Phoenix bird) Mk. 910A, E.V., c. 1850

LINCOLN'S HOUSE
Made by Petrus Regout

This is a souvenir plate from the celebration of the Abraham Lincoln centennial on February 12, 1909.

It shows the great President's home in Springfield, Illinois, and an oval insert bears his portrait. The border consists of a large wreath of lilies, roses, leaves and forget-me-nots on a dark field enclosed in a zig-zag edging.

Dutch, marked as above, with Maastricht, L.V., c. 1909

LONDON

Made by Powell, Bishop & Stonier

This scalloped plate carries a rim design of pairs of square crosses accented by white squares placed on a cobalt background.

Across the left center of the well is an oblong inset showing the buildings of Parliament and the Thames River on which there are several small boats afloat at the 'ower right. The Houses of Parliament consist of the House of Lords, which is on the side facing the river, and the House of Commons which is on the right. The tower at left is Victoria Tower, and the clock tower at the extreme left contains Big Ben, the famous clock bell.

The picture is placed against a flowering branch of a tree, a large bird flies at right, and a small insect is placed below the bird.

English, marked P. B. & S. Registered date Jan. 1882, Mk. 3137, L.V., c. 1882

MARINE

Made by The Mayer Pottery Co.

A sailboat is predominant on this picture plate. The entire surface of the dish is covered with a design of sky and sea and flying gulls. In the distance one can discern land, a windmill, and another small sailboat. The edge is scalloped and gilded. The plate was designed for display and is not part of a dinner set.

American, marked J. & E. Mayer, Mks. 30 to 38 Thorne, L.V., c. 1885.

MEDIAEVAL
Made by William Brownfield & Son

These two plates present a contrast in mediaeval life. On the first a lady tends her rose bushes within the confines of a castle wall. She is jewelled and elegantly gowned.

On the other a peasant cuts wheat with his scythe. His clothing is rough home spun, and his water canteen hangs from his belt. Part of a stone wall and part of a wooden fence define his background, and mark him as a serf laboring to bring in the harvest from the fields of his master.

English, marked W.B. & Son, Mk. 665, M.V., c. 1877

MONTILLA
Made by Davenport

This old plate is twelve sided and the rim is panelled. It is printed in a greyish blue. Five small pairs of flowers are placed on a background of circular lines and are separated by a pattern of foliated scrolls. The well is encircled by a ring of little scrolls containing X marks. Under these are tiny scrolls that give a spear point effect.

The center design depicts a quasi-religous structure at the right which is surmounted by an onion shaped tower. A statue can be seen in a gothic niche midway in the building. A lake separates the above structure from other buildings which are placed in the left center and left center distance. There are tall trees at the left front.

English, marked with printed name and impressed dated Anchor, Mk. 1181A, E.V., c. 1844

MOORISH PALACE

Maker Unknown

This coupe shaped plate is scalloped and the gilt edge is embossed with foliated scrolls. The sloping rim is fluted with lines that swirl toward the well.

The picture covers the entire dish and depicts a large castle, like the Alhambra, with domed roofs and minaret towers. It is placed against a setting of high mountains and overlooks a lake formed by a large waterfall that descends from the mountains in the background.

The foreground is occupied by several people in caftans and flat caps who stand beside a large tiered fountain. Behind them there is a railed terrace where people are bending over a child. Tall trees frame the picture on either side.

There is no mark on this plate and this name is used for cataloguing.

The same scene was used by John Wedge Wood on PERUVIAN. (Page 102, this book)

MOREA

Made by J. Goodwin

This plate has fourteen sides and is paneled. The edge is delineated with a dark band and a fine white line. The rim is decorated with poppies, foliated scrolls, and ribbon bound angular designs. The small flowers and ends of the scrolls descend the sides of the well.

The center picture is the usual Greco Roman dream-like scene with columned ruins and an arched bridge over a lake or stream. At center foreground there are three figures standing on a large rock and pointing towards the ruins. A tall tree rises at the extreme left.

English, marked as above and impressed Ironstone, (pattern registered in 1878), M.V., c. 1878.

MORRISIAN

Made by Doulton & Co.

The collar design on this pitcher and that on the base and handle consists of grape leaves on a scrolled background.

The picture on one side of the vessel shows a court scene of a woman in a long robe who is curtesying to a man who is dressed as a courtier would be at the time of King Charles of England. He has long hair, wears tall boots, a draped tunic coat with large collar and carries a long cane or rod. The scene on the opposite side show women dancing, they are dressed in fancy skirts and bodices and resemble gypsies.

(This name is derived from the old English word Morris which means to dance.)

English, marked as above, Mk. 1333, L.V., c. 1902.

MOUNTAIN STREAM

Made by J. & G. Meakin

This scenic wall plaque is slightly scalloped and is embossed with six scroll designs, which are slightly touched with gold. The picture covers the entire plate and shows a hut high in the Alpine Mountains. It is set beside a rushing stream.

English, marked as above, Mk. 2602, L.V., c. 1891.

NORFOLK
Made by Royal Doulton

The rim of this plate is printed with three vignettes, one of sailboats at sea, the second of a countryside church, and the third of windmills in fenced fields and farm land. These are divided by triangular cartouches formed of foliated scrolls and containing small flowers.

The central picture is of a large windmill tower standing high on a wooded bank overlooking the sea.

The fertile agriculture region of Norfolk, England, lies on a peninsula in the North Sea and consists of partly drained marsh land.

English, Mk. 1332, L.V., c. 1891.

NORTHERN SCENERY
Made by W. Adams & Co.

One side of this pitcher is printed with a mountain scene of tall trees and a lake with sailing ships; the other depicts a small castle on the lake shore. The collar is bordered with floral designs set in arches separated by small reserves filled with treillage.

This pattern was first issued by John Meir. The scenes differ on the various pieces of the set, but all depict landmarks of interest that are situated in Scotland. This particular scene is titled "Loch Creran with Barcaldine Castle".

English, marked as above, like mark 31, L.V., c. 1891.

OLD CURIOSITY SHOP
Made by Ridgways

The first three pictures illustrate that the scenes differ on the pieces of china available in this pattern. The handled dish shows a church set in the countryside, the plate depicts children at play under a tree, and the pitcher bears a scene of a woman standing by a stream. The border in all cases is composed of feathery vertical scrolls placed against a dotted diaper background joined by festoons of small flowers and leaves. These plates are marked with the famous Humphrey's Clock trademark. According to a letter received from the Ridgways Potteries Limited the design and trademark was originally used by William Ridgway & Son. Charles Dickens' story entitled "Humphreys Clock" had first appeared in a weekly paper in 1838. The picture of a platter in light greyish blue that we show here is so marked by W. R. Son & Co. and is one of those referred to in the letter from the pottery. It shows a canal scene, a man on a mule on a tow path is pulling a flat-boat through the canal and a party of people on board are drinking from mugs.

The pattern was reintroduced around 1900 and the same trade mark was used; the pattern was discontinued about 1930. The letter also states that most pieces are marked with impressed date numbers, for example 9 and 11 would represent September 1911. The first three examples photographed are labeled "Scenes from Charles Dicken's Old Curiosity Shop".

English, marked W.R.S. & Co. England, like mark 3309, L.V., c. 1910.

PARTHENON

Made by John Ridgway

The collar of this water pitcher is decorated with a very wide band of foliated scrolls and roses leaves and tendrils.

The scene on the body pictures a columned ruined three story building at the extreme right. At left there is a terrace with balustrades and a tall gyser fountain. In the center there is a lake with mountains behind it in the distance. The foreground is dominated by a large stone urn at the right. It is filled with vines and sprigs. Beneath it there are overscaled roses and tall trees rise between it and the ruin.

The pedestal base is without trimming and the panelled mold is left to be its own decoration.

English, Mk. 3257, E.V., c. 1845

PALERMO

Made by Joseph Clementson

This plate is twelve sided and the rim is paneled. A design of stylized lilies and tendrils is printed in greyish blue over a very dark background. This is contained by a row of small foliated scrolls.

The central scene is Swiss. There is an elaborate chalet at right, which is situated on a lake. At left is a fence and very tall trees. In the distance there are other buildings and towers.

This dish is slightly flown and should be classified as borderline.

English, marked as above, Mk. 910A, E.V., c. 1840.

101

PASTORAL
Made by Davenport

The slightly scalloped outer edge of this plate is bordered with a printed band of egg and beads. The rim design is composed of classical motifs of elongated acanthus leaves placed over a triangle made up of holly leaves. These are inverted as an alternate pattern. The well is also surrounded by an egg and bead band.

The central picture show three people and a dog. A man and two women are seen on a grassy bank. The man is playing a flute and one woman carries a basket as the other picks flowers. The background shows tall trees, a winding stream, and a square castle tower in the far distance. The backstamp gives no title to pattern, this name is used in order to catalogue the design.

English, marked as above, like mark 1194, M.V., c. 1870.

PERUVIAN
Made by John Wedge Wood

This octagonal vegetable dish is printed in slate blue and the upper part of the rim is slanted and paneled. The entire rim is printed with a pattern of four foliated scroll cartouches at the corners. Between these are three reserves framed by the scrolls. In each a flower is printed over a background of horizontal lines which form a net.

The center scene is Islamic and consists of a mosque situated on a lake at left. It has minerets and domes which rise against a background of tall mountains. In the foreground there are a railed terrace and a tall tree at right. In the left foreground near a fountain there is a group of costumed figures. In the far center distance a waterfall cascades into the lake.

English, marked J. Wedgwood and Ironstone, Registry Date May 1849, Mk. 4276A, E.V., c. 1849.

102

RABBITS

Made by Doulton & Co.

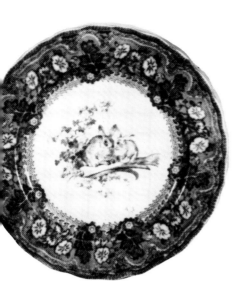

This scalloped plate has a swirled rim that is printed with morning glories and oak leaves on a field of soft cloth-like blue. The outer edge is detailed with a band of little hooked scrolls and a row of roses and foliated cornucopia designs placed over the oak leaf pattern. The bottom of the leaves enter the well and are part of a wreath of sprigs, scrolls and small flowers that circle the central design.

A pair of rabbits crouch on a small log and are sheltered by some leaves at the left, in the main design. The pattern is untitled, so this name will be used to catalogue the design.

English, marked as above, both printed and impressed, Mk. 1333, L.V., c. 1910.

ROMANCE

Maker Unknown

This is a picture of a little plate. Its border is deeply scalloped and heavily embossed. The rim bears three large cartouches enclosed in foliated scrolls, each bearing a design of two plumes and a pendant.

The center scene is dominated by a castle with three towers and a high arch that is placed in the background of the picture. There is a balustrade across the middle ground and an urn is placed on its right end. There is a covered urn in the left foreground and a New Zealand pine tree is at the center front.

There is no backstamp on the plate. This name is used to catalogue the pattern until the correct designation is learned.

RUINS

Made by Copeland

The plate photographed is unevenly scalloped and a dark line is placed around the outer edge. The border is printed with oak leaves and acorns. Some of these enter the well at six points.

The central scene covers the well and depicts a large castellated building, with towers and arches, that has fallen into ruins. There are bushes and trees growing in the court yard and against the tall walls. Clouds are pictured above this, a lake is in the center and a small flower-carpeted grassy area is in the foreground.

English, marked as above and also "Late Spode", Mk. 1068, Dated January 15, 1848. E.V. c. 1848

RUSKIN

Made by Ford & Sons

The scalloped beaded edge of this plate is printed in a dark blue. Six large triangular dark forms containing shells, fleur-de-lis and foliated scrolls are placed around the rim. These are separated by six triangular white areas containing stylized flowers and leaves. The well is outlined by a row of embossed beading.

The central scene shows a large house set in a country scene; perhaps a representation of the home of John Ruskin, the great English social reformer and writer, who lived at "Brantwood" on Conistan Lake until his death in 1900.

English, marked F. & Sons, Burslem, Mk. 1585 L.V., c. 1893

ST. PETERSBURG

Made by W. Adams & Co.

At the turn of the century this rose bordered plate was sold as a souvenir of a visit to the Florida West Coast City. It is printed in a greyish blue ink, with scenes of the main street, complete with horsedrawn carts and trolley cars, a sea side boardwalk and a fence made of shells.

English, marked as above, Mk. 27, L.V., c. 1891.

SCENES OF QUEBEC

Made by Frank Beardmore & Co.

Souvenir plates were made in England and distributed to other countries. This plate was sent to Canada, to a distributor in St. Johns, New Brunswick.

The plate celebrates the glories of the City of Quebec. The six reserves around the rim depict various famous scenic highlights in and near the city. The central scene shows the bluff upon which the city was built, as seen from the St. Lawrence river.

English, marked as above, Mk. like 307a, L.V., c. 1910.

STAG ISLAND

Made by Frank Beardmore & Co.

Greyish blue ink has been used to print this souvenir coupe shaped plate. The edge design is composed of stylized bell flowers.

The center scene shows a large pavilion on a lake shore and above this is depicted the head of a stag framed by a large foliated cartouche that is flanked with roses.

English, marked as above, Mk. like 307a, L.V., c. 1910.

SWISS

Made by Ralph Stevenson and Son

The teapot photographed has a deep collar design of floral tapestry inset with small ovals. A row of floral sprigs is set beneath this.

The scene on the body depicts a lake. In the foreground and at right is a large chalet with balconies and a fancy roof with crockets and carved eaves. A bridge decends from its porch and leads to a flowered island at the left on which tall trees are growing. In the background one can see other houses and towers. Part of this scene is reproduced on the spout. The base is trimmed with a circle of little sprigs.

English, marked R.S. & S., Mk. 3706, E.V., c. 1835.

SYLVAN

Made by Brown-Westhead, Moore & Co.

On the rim of this unevenly scalloped plate, there are four scenes of a castle set in the countryside; these alternate with four groups of stylized bell-flowers and leaves, joined in the center with a gothic scroll. The outer edge is bordered with a narrow blue band that has leaves twining around it over the picture of the castle.

In the center picture the castle appears in the background. In the foreground there are cattle grazing on the flowery bank of a stream and in the shade of tall graceful trees. Clouds above the castle towers complete the circular scene.

English, marked B.W.M. & Co., Cauldon, Mark 684, L.V., c. 1900.

SYRIA

Made by R. Cochran & Co.

The rim of this old dish is printed with six cartouches separated by a scrolled post design. Three of the reserves contain a scene of a building with a fancy pointed roof and tall palm trees. The other three contain a bouquet of wild roses. There is beading printed over the top of the design and fringe is printed at the bottom. This fringe follows the cartouches baroque forms which are placed so that they enter the well area.

The central scene is the usual European romantic one. A tall gothic spired building is at left, an elm rises at right. In the foreground there is a group of five persons in peasant costume. In the distance there are towers and mountains.

Scottish, marked R.C. & Co., Mk. 965, E.V., c. 1846

THEBAN
Made by F. & R. Pratt

The flange on this deep dish is unevenly scalloped and it is decorated with dark reserves containing vases decorated with a griffin or a deer in flight. These reserves are joined by acanthus leaves and scrolls.

The center of the well contains a picture of two vases, the one in the foreground is dark and large and has handles. It is decorated with a picture of two women in Greek costume. The other vase is at the left in the middle ground. It is covered and bears a design of running deer. The circular scene is completed by the branches and fronds of three tropical trees. Thebes was an ancient city-state in Greece, about forty miles north of Athens. It was destroyed by Alexander the Great, was rebuilt in 316 but Turkey gained control of the city and it was finally razed in 1311.

English, marked F. & R. P. & Co., Mk. 3144, E.V., c. 1845

TOWER
Maker Unknown

The border of this dish is printed with various flowers on a dark ground. The well is encircled by a spear point design.

The central picture shows a stone building in the center. It is surmounted by a tall round tower with a conical top. In the foreground there are a lake and a flowering, grassy bank. Tall trees are placed on each side of the scene. Except for the building all the design elements in the picture are somewhat stylized.

There is no backstamp on this plate. This name was given in order to catalogue the dish.

An example has been located with a different border marked R & M Co. Rowland & Marcellus were New York importers.

TURKEY
Made by Ridgways

The game plate pictured has the typical gadroon edge featured by this firm. The border is printed with large flowers joined by scrolls and sprigs to a heart shaped and lobed design composed of scrolls. The bottoms of all these elements enter the well.

The center picture is that of a wild turkey standing in a grassy field. A smaller bird is in the right background, and there is part of a broken fence at the left.

English, marked as above. Mk. 3316, L.V., c. 1900.

U.S.S. NEW YORK
Made by The French China Co.

An old American battleship is pictured at sea in the center of this scalloped deep tray. The border is very dark cobalt and gold lustre has been placed around the edge. The blue fades into the center scene which is defined by a painted gold scalloped line and fleur-de-lis.

American, marked "La Francais", (see Thorn p. 126) Mk. 24, L.V., c. 1890

VALENCIA

Made by Sampson Hancock & Sons

The edge of this bowl is scalloped and is embossed with a wreath of leaves over a white band. Lustre has been sprayed over this. The rim design consists of foliated cartouches containing a swag of roses. These are separated by a design that incorporates a floral and scrolled lobe at the top and a semicircular stylized design below. A ring of gold encircles the well. Below this are placed spear points and floral swags.

The central scene is the usual vista of marble railings, tall trees, and an urn filled with plants. In the foreground are two couples and a pair of greyhounds, one dog is dark and the other is very light.

English, marked "British Manufacture", and S.H.&S. Like Mk. 1933, L.V. c. 1910

English, marked S.H.&S. and Mk. 1933 L.V. c. 1910

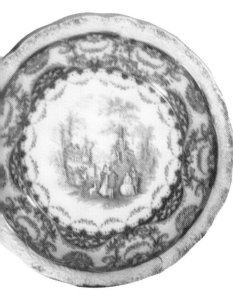

VENETIAN SCENERY

Made by W. Adams & Co.

The bowl photographed is in very poor condition. It has browned with age, and is crazed and cracked. It is difficult to ascertain how much the blue is flown and not merely blurred. However, the reverse side is flown.

The fluted rim is printed with large flowers in four scenic vignettes placed over a net background.

The central scene is bucolic and shows a towered building' at the left. There are tall trees at right. In the foreground there are cattle grazing on the leafy bank of a river or lake.

The only remote connection with Venice is a boat, which is not a gondola, in which there are two persons. There is also an arched bridge and there are mountains in the distance.

English, like Mark 28, L.V., c. 1900.

VIRGINIA
Made by J. & G. Meakin

This sauce dish is unevenly scalloped and the edge is detailed by scrolled embossing and dotted small swags. The border is printed with three reserves containing a picture of a large towered building, a lake and trees. These are separated by leafy garlands superimposed on a horizontal linear pattern. The well is detailed by a wreath of sprigs.

The central scene is the usual romantic combination of costumed people in the foreground standing on a terrace that has stone parapets and which overlooks a lake and is shadowed by tall trees. In the distance there are large castle-like towered buildings.

English, marked as above, Like the lower part of Mk. 2601, L.V., c. 1891.

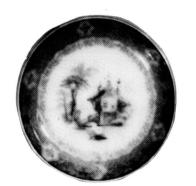

WARWICK
Made by Podmore Walker & Co.

The rim of this saucer is printed with six small cartouches that enclose a double handled vase form. These are set in a field of foliated scrolls. The well is encircled with a wreath of tiny flowers and sprigs.

The central scene is the usual romantic chalet-type house with spires and fancy eaves. In the center there is a sloping bridge over a stream which leads to a small island on which there are tall trees.

English, marked as above, Mk. 3075, E.V., c. 1850.

110

SCENIC CATEGORY
ADDENDA AND CORRECTIONS TO BOOK I

Page 62 **"COBURG"** *Re the mark, the word "warranted" in small straight letters is impressed on the back; this is one of the marks used by Edwards.*

Page 64 **"GENEVESE"** *Sam Laidacker in his book "Anglo American China", Vol. I, shows a blue pattern very similar to this and attributes it to Ridgway. The border is also a floral, but the band around the well is not present.*

Page 65 **"GOTHA"** *Prince Albert, consort to Queen Victoria, was the Prince of Saxe-Coburg and Gotha.*

Page 65 **"GOTHIC"** *The center scenes vary slightly on different size plates, bowls, and hollow ware. The border, of course, remains the same.*

Page 69 **"LEICESTER"** *At a recent antique show several pieces of this pattern were shown, including a platter that contains a central medallion. This is a large circular wagon wheel motif that is enclosed in a wide band that echoes the design on the rim.*

Page 71 **"MALTA"** *This example of the pattern should be classified borderline.*

Page 71 **"McNETTE"** *The original photograph was donated by a dealer and it has not been possible to secure another example.*

page 72 **"OLD CASTLE"** *Re the*  *mark, this mark has appeared with "Germany", so m... not be W & E Corn. Since the letters B & L are impressed into the plate, this was po... sibly the work of Burgess & Leigh who used such an impressed hall mark.*

page 74 **"RHONE"** *The center scenes differ. We show cut out from 8" plate.*

page 75 **"TIVOLI"** *This example is borderline.*

page 77 **"VIGNETTE"** *Should read made by J. Dimmock & Co.*

page '78 **"VISTA"** *The picture of this little match holder, or tooth pick, is used to show a... example of the pattern wherein the scene is definitely flown and the details are barel... distinguishable. The border is somewhat different from the one shown on the platte... in the book and consists of small flowers. It is also marked "Masons" and just the crown part of the mark is used. This was often done on the smaller pieces of a pattern.*

page 78 **"WALMER"** *This was the name of the British castle where Queen Victoria took he... child Prince Albert on a visit to the Duke of Wellington in 1842.*

ge 79 **"WASHINGTON VASE"** *The platter photographed is in the author's collection.*

ge 80 **"WATTEAU"** *(Doulton) Examples of this pattern have turned up with the border design only; that is, they contain no central scene.*

ge 82 **"WILD ROSE"** *Note that the description should read "a river scene and men are* **punting** *flat boats". (Punting means to propel a small boat by thrusting against the river bottom with a pole.)*

ge 82 **"ACADIA"** *This twelve sided deep dish is paneled and the rim is covered with a pattern of large shield forms composed of scrolls that terminate in a pair of large loops at the top, and which are connected by a fan shape. The outer edge is detailed with a narrow band of a small diaper pattern. The six spaces between the larger pattern are filled with a key-hole design.*

The center medallion is asymetrical and is heraldic in trim. The central scene shows a boat with a very high prow.

Acadia was the land of Evangeline who was French Hugenot. These people were driven from Canada by the British, who renamed the area Nova Scotia. The Hugenots fled by boat and went down the Mississippi to Louisiana.

There is no backstamp on the dish so it cannot be attributed, only the name is given, but it is probably early, 1850-70.

page 82 **"ATALANTA"** *This is the only example that has turned up in this pattern. The des*
appears only as a border and consists of oval medallions that contain one large dah
which alternates with cartouches of foliated scrolls containing groups of small dahli
The well is encircled by a wreath of small flowers and leaves.

This is probably another example like those of "Watteau" by Doulton and "Fa.
Villas" by Adams, in that some of the pattern was made without a center scene. I
important to collectors to recognize the border patterns, so we include this examp
English marked, like mark 4059, L.V., c. 1906.

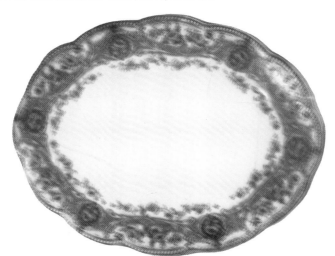

page 82 **"ATHENS"** *(W. Adams & Sons). This plate is fourteen sided and is printed in sl*
blue. The outer rim is detailed with five cartouches, each containing a picture of
eastern scene of temples and domed towers and surrounded by fancy scrolls. The
five pictures are joined by a flowered design at the top edge and a gothic trefoil a.
arch design at the bottom. The latter encircles the well and effects a spear po
wreath.

The central scene is dominated by a tall fountain basin mounted on a scrolled pedes.
and surmounted by a cupid holding a basin overhead. Two swans are placed in t.
water at the center left. In the background are columned temples and towering tre
English, marked as above, Mk. 23, Dated January 3, 1849, E.V., c. 1849

ge 83 **"RHONE SCENERY"** *A Flow Blue example has not been found, but one of my corresponding dealers reports that he has an example in soft bluish grey. We show a picture of a vegetable dish so that the reader can see the border design. The center scene is not the same as that described in the first book, in fact this scene is almost venetian in its details. The scenes differ on the plates and dishes and hollow ware, so it is important to recognize the rim pattern. The plate, also shown, depicts a man punting a high prowed boat in the foreground. A tall spired gothic building is at right and tall elm trees are at left. In the distance there is a castle-like structure. Clouds complete the circular scene.*

page 83 **"TEMPLE"** *This dish is twelve sided, the rim is slightly panelled and is covered with a design of Gothic scrolls against a dark ground on the upper half, and a row of vertical lines and quatrefoils on the lower half. A wreath of small flowers encircles the bottom of the rim and is succeeded by a row of small spear point design around the slope of the well.*

The scene in the center of the plate depicts columned temples, the larger surmounted by a statue; these are situated at the left and overlook a lake. At right there is a very large urn on a pedestal, a railed parapet, and tall gracefall trees. In the foreground there is the top of a broken column, and five people dressed in tunics are on the lake shore nearby.

PLATE XI

Teasets reading from top to bottom: 1st. Kremlin with Whampoa sucrier; 2nd. Oregon by Mayer; 3rd. Scinde; 4th. Chapoo with Rock sugar bowl; bottom, Amoy with Amour creamer. Shown for purpose of comparing hollow ware shapes. (See Folio of Drawings for additional shapes.) Note: Potteries did not limit themselves to one shape in a popular pattern, and did use different molds to suit popular demand.

Floral Category

ALBERTA

Made by Ridgways

This plate has an outer edge of printed dots. Next a plain band encircles the rim. This is interrupted by a double Greek key design at six points.

Full blown roses with buds and leaves are placed between the Greek key patterns and all elements of the design are joined by swags of sprigs and small flowers. Leaves from the roses enter the well.

English, marked as above, Mk. 3312, L.V., c. 1910

ALMA

Made by William Adderly

This gilt edged plate is entirely covered with a design of large poppies, buds, and leaves.

English, marked as above, Registry mark #365822, Mk. 49, L.V., c. 1900

APSLEY PLANT

Made by Burgess & Leigh

This wavy edged plate is decorated at the top of the rim with a circle of connected scrolls. Three elongated sprays of lilies alternate around the rim with a small pendant design.

The center is a flower with large geranium-type leaves.

English, marked B&L, Mark 712, M.V., c. 1862

ARGYLE

Made by Myott, Son & Co.

This floral pattern, consisting of poppies, leaves and buds covers the sides of the teapot photographed. The rim is scalloped, embossed with vertical lines, covered with cobalt, as are the spout and the handle. No foot rim is visible on the pot, and the bottom of the body is scalloped.

English, marked M.S. & Co., Stoke, Mk. 2809, L.V., c. 1898

ASTER

Made by the Upper Hanley Company

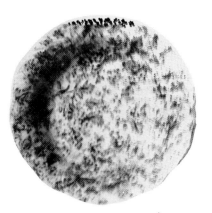

This is an example of an all-over pattern. The weaving stems, flowers, leaves, and buds cover the scalloped, embossed bowl photographed, and gold luster has been placed over the sprawling design.

English, marked as above, Mark 3928, L.V., c. 1895

ASTORIA

Made by the New Wharf Pottery

This unevenly scalloped plate has a beaded edge outlined by a light blue band. It is also embossed with a filigree of net and flowers.

Three small bouquets of flowers are placed around the rim, and these alternate with a pair of the same little flower.

English, marked as above, Mk. 2886, L.V., c. 1891

ATLAS
Made by W. H. Grindley and Company

The wash basin photographed has an edge that is scalloped and embossed. The narrow rim is decorated with sprigs and ribbons and these are contained by a narrow dark band. The body is printed with large flowers.

The unusual detail of this pattern is found in the cobalt fluted hexagon that surrounds the central picture of roses and leaves. This same dark area is used at the bottom of both the pitcher and tooth brush holder in this set.

English, marked as above, Mk. 1842, L.V., c. 1891

AVON
Made by Keeling & Co.

This relish dish is scalloped, embossed with fluting and heavily gilded. The design is floral and appears mostly on the rim. Some sprays of the sweetpea-type flower do enter the well at one side of this dish.

English, marked Late Mayer, Mk. 2243, L.V., c. 1900

AZALEA
Possibly made by John Leigh

The top of the collar on this wash pitcher is scalloped and gilded. Gold lustre is placed over the design. Wave-like swirl embossings are on both collar and body.

The flower pattern of azaleas and leaves almost covers the pitcher.

Edward Bourne and J.E. Leigh became Bourne and Leigh in 1892. This mark must predate their merger.

English, marked J.E.L., L.V., c. 1885

122

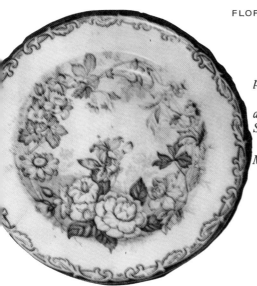

BALMORAL

Made by Mann & Co.

The edge of this plate is embossed and printed with outlined scrolls.

The floral design covers the entire well and consists of many different flowers. Shadow tracery fills in the background.

English, marked as above, Mk. 2498, M.C., c. 1860

BAVARIA

Maker Unknown

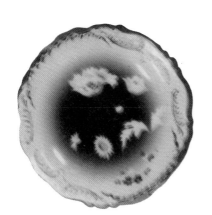

The edge of this small shallow porcelain dish is fluted, scalloped and embossed.

An unusual use of flow blue has been obtained by placing the deepest cobalt in the center of the dish, and letting this fade out to the edge.

White areas have been reserved for a sort of silhouetted flowers and leaves.

Small forget-me-nots are printed on one side of the rim. Gold has been placed over the embossing. There is no name on the back. This name is used to catalogue the pattern.

Bavarian, marked B & K, Probably L.V., c. 1891

BEGONIA

Made by Gibson & Sons Ltd.

This little scalloped and embossed hairpin tray is entirely blue and a pattern of begonias and leaves is printed in the center.

English, marked G & S Ltd, Mk. 1679a, L.V., c. 1905

BELFORT

Made by John Maddock & Sons Ltd.

This little relish dish is printed in slate blue. It is scalloped and the handles are embossed. The baroque design consists of rolls and treillage and small flowers, appearing only on the rim.

English, marked as above, Mk. 2464, L.V., c. 1896

BELMONT

Made by Alfred Meakin

The lid of a covered vegetable dish is photographed here. It is scalloped, embossed and dark edged.

Groups of flowers are placed around the rim composed of a large wild rose surrounded by leaves and sprigs. The design is basically triangular with the point toward the center of the dish.

English, marked as above, Mk. 2586, L.C., c. 1891

BERLIN GROUPS

Made by W. Adams & Sons

The teapot pictured is made in a classic, simple shape. The pattern consists of groups of large flowers; dahlias with large shaggy single leaves, and five petalled aster-like blossoms.

It is somewhat like "Claremont Groups."

English, marked as above, Mk. 22, like Mk. 24, M.V., c. 1860

BOLINGBROKE (THE)
Made by Ridgways

This gravy tray has the scalloped, embossed, gadroon edge typical of Ridgway and the printing is in the soft dark blue characteristic of this firm. The border design is composed of swags of roses and buds on a dark background. Some of the buds and leaves enter the well.

The name "Bolingbroke" refers to a castle of that name in which Henry Bolingbroke, who later became Henry IV of England, was born.

English, marked as above, Mk. 3313, dated, L. V., c. 1909.

BORDEAUX
Made by Vielliard & Co.

This scalloped dish is printed with large morning glories and pansies over a rim pattern of fine dotted net. The floral designs enter the well which is almost covered with leaves and buds and tendrils.

French, marked, A. Vielliard and Porcelaine and Vielliard & Co. on three intertwined crescents, Probably M.V., c. 1865

BOTANICAL
Made by Charles Meigh

This baroque plate is heavily embossed with foliated scrolls. The upper rim is printed with a beige line outlined in cobalt interrupted at six points by scrolled cartouche forms. Much gilt has been used on this border.

The central bouquet is in soft colours of rose, lemon yellow, pale orange and a vibrant light green. The lower stems and leaves are done in cobalt and gold.

English, marked "Opaque Porcelain", marked CM (and a printed Chinese mark), Mk. 2614a, E. V., c. 1842

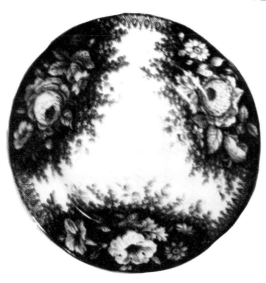

BOUQUET

Made by August Nowotny & Co.

Three large groups of different cultivated flowers are printed on this shallow bowl. They are joined by a gothic type narrow band composed of triangles ending in a cross and oval pendants. The floral designs cover most of the dish leaving only a small triangular area in the middle.

This pattern has also been found with English marks, a Royal Coat of Arms and Imperial Ironstone China, London, which resembles marks used by Birks Brothers and Seddon, 1877-1886.

German, marked as above, (see Thorne, pg. 26, Mk. 9), M.V., c. 1877

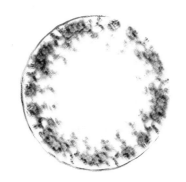

BROOKLYN

Made by Myott, Son & Co.

This gently scalloped plate has wave and scroll embossing.

The design consists of anemones and forget-me-nots linked by scrolls. Sprays of small leaves and forget-me-nots enter the upper part of the well.

English, marked as above, Mk. 2810, L.V. c. 1900

BYZANTINE

Made by Wood & Son

This soup dish is unevenly scalloped and is printed on a shell embossed blank like that used by New Wharf Pottery for "Waldorf." The outer edge and the shells are covered in dark blue.

The border design is asymetrical and has a large spray of prunus and a peony on one side that enters one third of the way into the well. There are two smaller sprigs of prunus opposite the large design.

English, marked as above, Mk. 4285, L.V., c. 1900

CHATSWORTH
Made by Ford & Sons

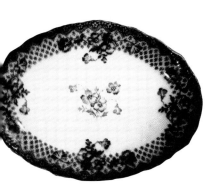

This platter is printed in slate blue. It is scalloped and its outer edge is detailed with a row of small stylized roses and forget-me-nots enclosed in a scalloped border of scrolls and dots. The rim is printed with four groups of realistic primroses on each side of the rim and these are placed on a diapered field of small stylized five petaled flowers. The buds and leaves from the primroses enter the well and a small bouquet of the same flowers is placed in the center.

English, marked F & Sons Burslem, Mk. 1585, L.V., c. 1893

CHATSWORTH
Made by Myott, Son & Co.

The unevenly and deeply scalloped small platter shown has embossing of scrolls and flowers. Gold lustre has been placed over this, against a deep blue background.

The central design consist of a large bouquet of wild roses, buds and leaves and this covers the entire well.

English, marked as above, Mk. 2810, L.V., c. 1900

CHELTENHAM
Maker Unknown

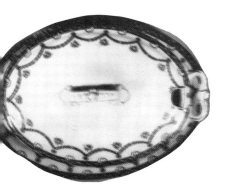

This small tureen is decorated around the gilded edge with a band that encloses little wavy scrolls and which is interspersed with scallop shell designs. Garlands of tiny bell flowers are attached to small stylized flowers around the upper rim. Below the swags created by the small flowers there are placed realistic small roses.

Probably English, probably L.V., c. 1900

CHINA ASTER

Possibly made by Skinner & Walker

The pattern of this platter depicts callistephus chinesis; the China Aster. It shows both the single and the multi-petalled varieties. The platter is basically octagonal and its edge is decorated with a spear point design.

English, marked (impressed) "Pearl Ware", Like Mk. 3569a, M.V., c. 1870

CHISWICK

Made by Ridgways

The soup plate pictured is printed with a very dark slate blue ink. Its edge is unevenly scalloped and heavily embossed with scrolls on an almost black ground that is touched up with gold.

The floral design apperas on the rim and consists of three equally spaced sprays of small flowers and leaves, part of which trails into the well. Single small flowers are placed between the three main elements.

English, marked as above, Mk. 3312, Registry #295284, L.V., c. 1900

CLEMATIS

Made by Samuel Barker & Son

The vase pictured is scalloped at the top and around the pedestal. Vary dark cobalt has been placed in these areas.

The design appears on the body of the vase and consists of realistic large clematis flowers and leaves.

English, marked S.B. & S., Mk. 263, M.V. c. 1870

128

CLEMATIS

Made by Johnson Bros.

The basin and pitcher shown are large and are part of a wash set. The edges of both pieces are decorated with cobalt and gilt lustre and both are fluted and embossed. The realistic clematis design shows clearly on the body of the pitcher.

English, marked as above, Mk. 2179, L.V., c. 1910

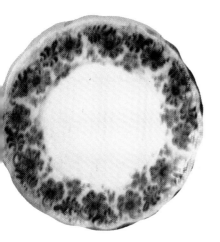

CLIFTON

Made by Ford & Son

This plate is unevenly scalloped and its edge is detailed with a heavy embossing of rounded palings and scrolls and grape-like clusters.

The design appears only on the rim and consists of a greyish blue printing of chrysanthemums, scrolls and sprays of small flowers. The latter enter the edge of the well.

English, marked F. & Sons, Mk. 1585, L.V., c. 1900

CLOVER

Made by Josiah Wedgwood & Sons

The edge of this plate is outlined with a row of wheat, and the rim is printed with a wreath of clover blossoms, leaves, sprays of wheat and ferns.

The center bouquet is made up of the same plants.

English, marked (impressed) "Pearl", Mk. 4086, dated 1860, M.V., c. 1860

COLESBERG

Made by Keeling & Co.

A lavender grey-blue ink has been used to print this pattern. The collar is deeply scalloped and heavily embossed and gilded. The design on the collar is composed of scrolls printed in a light blue against a dark background. The body of the vessel is divided into 3-inch sections of swirl vertical embossing. These sections are filled with a design of baroque scrolled trellis, roses and sprigs.

English, marked K & Co. and Late Mayer, Mk. 2243, L.V., c. 1886

COLONIAL

Made by Homer Laughlin China Co.

The edge of this scalloped plate is outlined first in white, then a narrow gold line and lastly a dark blue scrolled band. The rim, which is embossed with a scrolled design for three quarters of its depth, carries a pattern of bell flowers, daisies, leaves and scrolls. Some of the bell flowers enter the well.

American, Thorne (page 133), Mk. 28, L.V., c. 1880

COLWYN

Made by New Wharf Pottery

This scalloped gilt edged plate, bears a border design of dotted embossing and printed small scrolls.

The rim design is superimposed on a dotted field and consists of foliated scrolls and swags of forget-me-nots with five pendant shield floral designs.

The central medallion consists of a triangle of leaves surrounding a dotted field and encircled by forget-me-nots.

English, marked as above, Mk. 2886, L.V., c. 1891.

CONVOLVOLUS

Made by William Ridgway Son & Co.

This deep dish is edged with a small pointed design that gives a spear point effect.

The design covers the dish and consists of the flower that gives it the pattern name above. Convolvolus grows in the Mediterranean area. It is a trailing small plant whose little pinkish-purple flowers resemble morning glories.

English, marked WRS&Co., Mk. 3307, E.V., c. 1842.

CORONET

Made by Sampson Hancock & Sons

The edge of this saucer is unevenly scalloped and is outlined with a narrow band of vertical lines. There is some scroll embossing at six places on the rim and a wreath of embossing surrounds the well.

The pattern consists of five small crowns, surmounted by heraldic foliated leaves enclosed in scrolls and placed over a triple design of bell flowers. The coronets alternate with bouquets of mixed flowers. Swags of small roses and leaves join both design elements at the lower part of the rim.

English, marked SH&Sons, Registry #341031, Mk. 1933, L.V., c. 1906

DAMASK ROSE

Made by Davenport

The bottom part of a covered dish is photographed. The upper edge design consists of a narrow blue line and tiny leaves. The open work handles are gilded.

The flower that gives this pattern its name is depicted within three sprays on the rim of the dish, and in a bouquet in the center of the well.

English, marked as above, Mk. 1181A, Impressed anchor that is dated, M.V., c. 1860.

DERBY
Made by W. H. Grindley

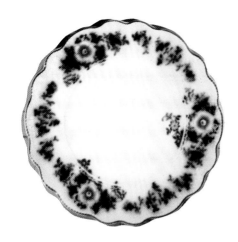

This pattern is made up of large flat anemone-type flowers placed in three spots around the rim. These flowers are painted in a henna red as are the buds that are placed among blue sprigs and leaves.

The edge of the plate is scalloped, gilded, beaded and embossed with small flowers. A lacey band of embossing on the lower rim surrounds the well.

English, marked as above, Mk. 1842, L.V., c. 1891.

DRESDON
Made by Johnson Bros.

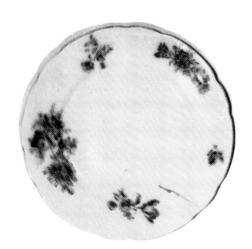

This plate is gently scalloped and is gilt edged.

Five groups of different flowers are placed around the rim. There are two sprays with leaves and buds and two pairs of flowers and a single bud.

This is a rendition of the antique pattern "Chantilly Sprigs".

English, marked as above, Mk. 2177, L.V., c. 1900.

DUCHESS
Made by Dunn Bennett

This pattern was misplaced in the Art Nouveau category in Book I on page 165. It is clearly a floral design. The scalloped edge of the dish is fluted and gilded.

Large dahlias are placed in the center of the plate and cover the well. Sprigs and light sprays radiate from these and cover the rim.

English, marked as above, Mk. 1422, L.V., c. 1900

DUNBARTON

Made by New Wharf Pottery

The tureen photographed is decorated with wreaths of shaggy aster-like flowers and leaves. One wreath surmounts the handle on the scalloped lid and the other encircles the body of the dish. The printing is done in greyish blue.

English, marked as above, Mk. 2886, L.V., c. 1891.

EASTERN FLOWERS

Made by Mellor, Venables & Co.

This fourteen sided saucer has an edging of dark blue and a criss cross design that gives a triangular effect.

The pattern is of different flowers; a peony, a chrysanthemum, a group of lilies and dahlias. These are placed around the rim and enter the well which is centered with a small bouquet.

English, marked as above, Mk. 2646 E.V., c. 1845

EGLANTINE

Made by Keller & Guerin

The saucer photographed shows the rim pattern divided into three groups.

On the plates in this design a double rose and bud pattern appear at four points. These are placed on a dark ground and are linked around the rim with a gothic ironwork design of long pointed hearts and by a field of mossy sprigs.

The center design is a single large stemmed rose and buds on the saucer and a pair of roses on the plates.

Eglantine is the name of one of the wild roses commonly called "sweet brier".

French, marked K & G Luneville, See Thorne (page 7, Mk. 2), L.V., c. 1891.

EGLANTINE

Made by Charles Meigh

This plate is unevenly scalloped and the outer edge is detailed with a ring of angled lines and dots.

Large foliated scrolls cover most of the rim. From these five large swags of different flowers enter the well and smaller swags and floral pendants are placed between them.

In the center there is a bouquet of eglantine, commonly called "sweet brier", a wild pink rose with brown stems covered with sharp hooked thorns. It has dark green leaves that grow close together. Both the flowers and leaves give a spicy fragrant scent.

English, marked CM, Mk. 2614a, E.V., c. 1840.

ELIZABETH

Maker Unknown

This pitcher bears no backstamp and it will be catalogued with the name of its owner.

The collar is deeply scalloped and is molded in half curves and embossed with fleur-de-lis.

Very large fleur-de-lis are placed at the base and balance the deep collar at top.

The body is panelled and is decorated on the sides with flowers. On the reverse side there are two wild roses and sprigs. On the side shown there are pansies, violets and large leaves.

Probably English, probably L.V., c. 1885

ELSIE

Made by New Wharf Pottery

This scalloped plate has wave and scroll embossing. The rim is patterned with bouquets and scrolled lattice that alternate with pairs of flowers and single scrolled floral forms. These enter partially into the well. At center there are two little flowers and some leafy sprays.

English, marked as above, Mk. 2886, L.V., c. 1891

ENGLISH ROSE
Maker Unknown

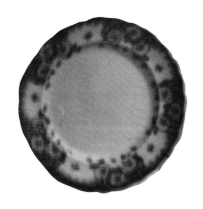

The dark edge of this plate is scalloped and gilded. The pattern appears on the rim only and consists of five triangular groups of three wild roses which alternate with a single small flower and a row of printed beading at the top edge of the rim. The bottom of the large groups enter the well and forms a wreath.

English, marked England, L.V., c. 1891.

FLORA
Possibly made by Cockson & Chetwynd

This little plate has twelve sides and the edge is outlined with a dark band and a printed leafy design. The rim is decorated with three sprays of small flowers that alternate with three sprigs.

The central design covers the well and is composed of dahlias with large buds.

Lustre has been placed over the flowers and around the edge.

English, marked C.C. & Co., Mark 976, impressed "Pearl" in a half circle, probably M. V., c. 1867.

FLORAL GROUPS
Maker Unknown

This is a tray to a small round sauce tureen. It is unevenly scalloped and heavily embossed at the pierced handles with flower and leaf shapes. These are outlined with gold and so is the edge.

The outer rim is trimmed with leaves and shaggy tulip-like flowers. Five different flowers appear on the panelled rim and a pair of poppies and leaves are placed in the center.

This is like the "Claremont Groups" and the "Berlin Groups" so this name will be used to catalogue until the correct identity is established.

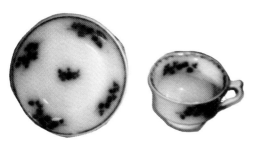

FORGET ME NOT
Maker Unknown

This is a picture of a child's cup and saucer. The upper inside edge of the cup and the outer edge of the saucer are decorated with a border of small scrolls.

This design resembles the hand painted stylized floral designs, but it is transfer printed.

Four groups of forget-me-nots are printed around the rim of the saucer and one small flower and fern spray is placed in the center. The same motifs are repeated in the cup.

There is no backstamp on either piece, this name is used to catalogue the pattern.

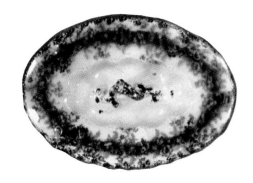

GARLAND
Made by W. & E. Corn

This is a picture of the top of a covered vegetable dish. The edge is slightly scalloped and embossed and is covered with gold lustre. The oval area around the handle is also scalloped and embossed.

A blue band encircles the rim and small shaggy flowers, forget-me-nots and sprigs are printed over this.

English, marked as above, Mk. 1113, L.V., c. 1904

GEM
Made by John Maddock & Sons Ltd.

This scalloped gilt edged plate is printed in a greyish blue. The outer edge has an embossed band and some scroll embossing. A wreath of small flowers at the top edge connects seven patterns of flowers and foliated scrolls. These are set on a net background and are connected at the bottom by scrolls and sprigs that form a wreath design around the top of the well.

English, marked as above, Mk. 2464, Registry #308970, L.V., c. 1896.

GERANIUM

Made by John Ridgway & Co.

The light edge of this platter is unevenly scalloped and is outlined by a dark blue band around the light band of foliated scrolls. There is heavy embossing at the four sides and this is overprinted with blue.

The large design in the center pictures the five-lobed geranium variety found in southern Europe.

English, marked I. Ridgway, Mk. 3256, Registered March 9, 1847, E.V., c. 1847

GLADIOLUS

Made by Doulton & Co.

The neck of this porcelain vase has a collar of gold filigree over cobalt blue. The handles and the base are also cobalt trimmed with gold.

A tall stalk of gladiolus in bloom appears on one side of the body and a drawing of buds and leaves is on the reverse side.

Gold lustre has been sprayed over the floral pattern.

English, marked as above, Mk. 1333, L.V., c. 1902

GLEN

Made by Sampson Hancock & Sons

The pattern on this unevenly scalloped plate is printed predominately on one side of the dish. Ferns and black eyed susans, dandelion puffs and tall slender weeds form the main design. At top and on the opposite side to the large grouping are small sprays of blossoms and sprigs.

English, marked as above, Mk. 1932, L.V., c. 1910

HAARLEM
Made by Villeroy & Boch

This simple design consists of tulips with small flowers and sprigs alternating with a pair of daisies.

One of the Villeroy & Boch potteries was at Wallerfagen in the Saar Basin.

German, marked V & B, M, Saar Basin, See Hartman (page 76, Mk. 32), also Cushion (page 210), L.V., pre 1891.

HAMPTON SPRAY
Made by W. H. Grindley

The edge of this plate is trimmed with a band that is interrupted at six places by a fleur-de-lis design.

The dish is unevenly scalloped and is rimmed with white beading. Lacy arched embossing covers the upper half of the rim. A large rose, leaves and a spray form is placed on one side of the rim. Opposite it is a smaller design of wild roses. The two are joined by a wreath of star shaped flowers and sprigs.

English, marked as above, Mk. 1842, L.V., c. 1891.

HARVEST
Made by Alfred Meakin Ltd.

The pattern on this plate is asymetrical and from the heavier part of the design a spray that resembles wheat crosses the well. The principal elements of the pattern are grape leaves, small flowers in clusters and corn flowers.

English, marked as above, Mk. 2587, L.V., c. 1907.

HARWOOD

Made by New Wharf Potteries

This bone dish is deeply scalloped. It is printed in black on a flown blue background with a pattern of garlands of scrolls and small bouquets of roses. On this example the design is on the rim only. Also the garlands have been embellished with gold paint.

English, marked as above, Mk. 2886, L.V., c. 1891.

ILFORD

Made by Keeling & Co., Ltd.

The small bowl photographed has large sprays of leaves and buds in two places around the body and a full flowered lily on its stem on the third part. Gold lustre has been sprayed over the pattern and a gold rim encircles the foot.

English, marked as above, Mk. 2243, Registry #571753, L.V., c. 1910

IRIS

Made by Pearl Pottery Co., Ltd.

This tall straight panelled vase with flared lip is printed with large vertical iris and leaves. The printing is done in two shades of dark cobalt against a pale blue background. Gold lustre has been placed profusely in the background.

English, marked P P & Co., Mk. 2983, L.V., c. 1910

KENDAL
Made by Ridgways

This gilt edged scalloped plate has light scroll and dot embossing. The rim is covered with five large full blown roses with buds and leaves.

English, marked as above, Mk. 3312, L.V., c. 1910

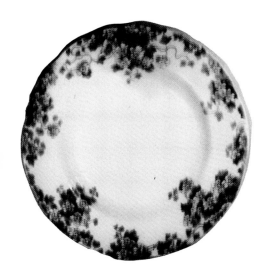

KENWOOD
Made by Alfred Meakin

The pattern on this scalloped soup plate is printed in a greyish blue, appears mostly on the rim and consists of three triangular groups of bramble roses, which alternate with smaller groups of the same flowers.

English, marked as above, Mk. 2483, L.V., c. 1891.

LADYBUG
Made by Davenport

This scalloped gold edged plate is porcelain and most of the body is swirled.

A large daffodil and other wildflowers form a bouquet on one side. A small spray of forget-me-nots is nearby and a fat ladybug is placed by itself opposite both designs.

No name is printed on the backstamp; this name is used to catalogue.

English, marked as above, Mk. 1194, M.V., c. 1870

140

LILY

Made by William Adderly and Company

The ovoid pomander jar photographed is used for the storage of rose petals in order to form a sachet.

Its collar and base are gold lustred and a large lily and leaves are printed on the side of the vessel.

The lid is perforated.

English, marked as above, Mk. 49, L.V., c. 1880

LILY

Made by Blackhurst & Tunnicliffe

The coffee pot pictured has a very dark collar and is printed with lilies and spear-shaped leaves. The same design appears around the bottom of the pot and on its spout and handle.

The design on the body consists of two rather formalized lilies with leaves, vine like stems and tendrils.

English, marked B & T, M.V., c. 1879

LILY

Made by Thomas Dimmock

This octagonal platter has a deep sloping panelled rim. Its edge is printed with a band composed of thick vine stems wound with tendrils.

The pattern consists of two very large spotted lilies, one on each side of the dish.

Small sprays of leaves and flowers are placed on the top rim.

In the center of the design the large dark leaves that form the base for the lily on the left, also form a base for a spray of ribbon grass and little flowers. A butterfly is perched on this grouping and a large insect flies above it.

English, marked "D", and "Kaolin Ware", . Exact Mark 1298, E. V., c. 1844

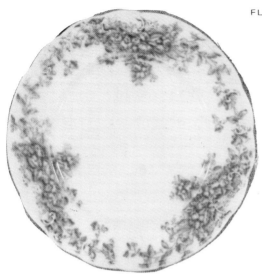

LILY

Made by Alfred Meakin

Three sprawling groups of lilies, leaves and small flowers are placed on the rim of this scalloped plate which is embossed with scrolls around the edge. The three floral groups, which are triangular in shape, enter the well at the bottom of the design and are joined on the upper rim by sprigs of small leaves and buds.

English, marked as above with Tunstall, Mk. 2581, L.V., c. 1885

LIMOGES

Possibly made by C. H. Brannam

The outer edge of this scalloped soup dish is decorated with a design of twisted rope. Four large pairs of peonies, buds and leaves and flowerets alternate with four little groups containing three daisy-like flowers. Parts of the larger designs enter the well.

English, marked CHB Co., L.V., c. 1891

LOTUS

Made by Cockson & Harding

The biscuit barrel photographed has a simple handle on its lid and a narrow gold line around the base. The pattern is named for the large flower and stem that appear in this picture. This reverse side bears a picture of a swallow.

English, marked C. & H. Tunstall, Mk. 979, M.V., c. 1860

LOUISE

Made by New Wharf Pottery

This unevenly scalloped saucer is enhanced with a row of ribbon embossing and is printed with a wreath of small lilies. The rim is decorated with vertically drawn lines of lilies and leaves and the well is encircled by a band of ribbon design. The central flowers are a pair of lilies with stalks and leaves. This printing is in slate blue.

English, marked as above, Mk. 2886, L.V., c. 1891

LUCANIA

Made by Edward Clarke & Co.

This soup plate is gently scalloped and is gilt edged. The design appears on the rim only and consists of trumpet-shaped flowers like morning glories, serrated leaves and little round buds.

English, marked Royal Semi Porcelain with B, probably Mk. 896, probably L.V., c. 1885

LYNTON

Made by The Ceramic Art Co.

The Ceramic Art Company of Hanley, England, were decorators for the pottery of the era, but also decorated wares made for themselves.

The pitcher and bowl photographed are gently scalloped. A large sprawling design of poppies, roses and violets with their various leaves, covers most of the pitcher and appears on the sides of the bowl.

English, marked as above, Mk. 828, Registry #276958, L.V., c. 1900

MABELLE
Made by Burgess & Leigh

The gilt edge of this plate is scalloped and is detailed with fluted embossing. Embossed scrolls on the rim define the pattern areas which consists of three long sprays of poppies which alternate with pairs of the same.

English, marked as above, Mk. 717, Registry #274526, L.V., c. 1910

MALLOW
Made by Boulton, Machin & Tennant

This pattern is of an herb that bears purple, pink or white flowers and has angular lobed or dissected leaves. A mallow rose is in the hibiscus family.

Probably English, probably M.V., c. 1855-60

MALO
Made by Samuel Alcock & Co.

This very large platter, 21-inches by 17-1/2-inches, has a slightly fluted rim which is outlined with a printed scalloped design composed of interlocking narrow lines. A spear-point effect is obtained by tiny scrolls and dots. The main design appears in the center of the well and is repeated on all four sides on a small scale. This a stylized drawing of Malo, probably Lanatera Trimestris, which is an herb of the malva genus. These are a common wild plant with angularly lobed leaves. Hollyhocks and hibiscus are related plants. The main design is surrounded by feathery smaller flowers and leaves.

English, marked SA & Co., Mk. 75, E.V., c. 1845

MARIGOLD

Maker Unknown

This is one of a pair of 13" tall vases. The one photographed has a deep cobalt collar and pedestal base.

The marigolds are printed in a very dark purplish blue on the body of the vase and gold lustre has been flecked over the pattern. The ornate gilded handles and embossing are typical of the middle Victorian era.

Probably English, M.V., pre 1891

MARLBOROUGH

Made by Wood & Son

The scalloped edge of this basin enhances the shape of the sides which are puffed out in rounded forms. These are decorated with a beaded horse shoe shape containing clumps of small flowers and trailing leaves and sprigs. The horse shoe shapes are separated by an embossed fleur-de-lis design.

English, marked as above, Mk. 4285, L.V., c. 1900

MATLOCK

Made by F. Winkle & Co.

The platter photographed has a dark cobalt edge that is contained within lighter blue foliated scrolls. Small flowers that resemble hawthorne are placed around the rim, each in a swirling embossed enclosure. Sprigs from these flowers enter the well.

English, marked F.W.& Co., Mk. 4213, L.V., c. 1890

MAY

Made by W. H. Grindley

This small soap dish is encircled on both lid and body with a pattern of carnations.

Another example of this pattern was found marked with a large green similar mark, so the dish may date after 1910.

English, marked as above, Mk. 1842, L.V., c. 1891

MEDWAY

Made by Alfred Meakin Ltd.

This plate is irregularly scalloped, and it is printed in a pale greyish blue. The rim pattern is contained at the top by a circle of scrolls and the outer edge is defined by a pattern of squiggles.

Three pairs of six petalled flowers are placed in oval cartouches around the rim. These alternate with small bouquets of the same flower. Forget-me-nots and garlands of tiny flowers link the two design elements.

English, marked as above, Mark 2582 L.V., C. 1897

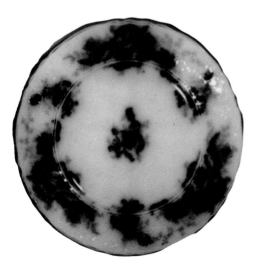

MENTONE

Made by Johnson Bros.

This unevenly scalloped plate has an indented edge and heavy wave-like embossing in three places on the rim.

Large sprays of ferns and a species of serrated daffodils are placed between the embossings. These are also separated by a smaller fern and scroll design. The bottom of both elements enter the well, and a single daffodil with ferns and sprigs is placed in the center of the dish.

English, marked as above, L.V., c. 1900

MILTON

Made by Wood & Sons

A pattern of various small flowers is printed on the rim of this unevenly scalloped gilt edged plate. The outer border is a continuous row of mossy sprigs. At five points the design descends toward the well in a triangular effect of leaves and sprigs.

This dish is flown on the reverse side, but the pattern may be borderline.

English, marked as above, Mk. 4283, Registry #233066, L.V., c. 1900

MORNING GLORY

Made by G. L. Ashworth & Bros.

This soup dish carries its large sprawling design of morning glories and leaves primarily on its flange, but a couple of flowers and leaves are depicted on the sloping sides of the well.

English, impressed Ashworth, Mk. 137, M.V., c. 1865

MORNING GLORY

Maker Unknown

This twelve sided dish is panelled and its outer edge is detailed with a very dark border contained within scrolls with small ivy leaves and little blossoms.

The bold large pattern of three different flowers, morning glories, lilies and daisies, covers most of the dish.

A small butterfly appears on the left rim.
Probably English, probably M.V., c. 1860

MOSS ROSE III

Made by Jacob Furnival & Co.

The name on the back of this dish is surrounded by a wreath and the initials J.F. & Co. are placed beneath this.

The dish is scalloped and embossed with foliated scrolls that are overprinted with cobalt.

Three moss roses are placed on the rim and these are separated by three bud forms.

The well is almost covered with a very large picture of a moss rose with its leaves and buds.

English, marked J.F. & Co., Mk. 1643, M.V., c. 1860.

NIAGARA

Made by Mellor, Taylor & Co.

The saucer pictured is unevenly scalloped and it is embossed near the edge with small swags and scrolls.

The design appears only on the rim on the saucer photographed. A pair of scrolls with small fleur-de-lis and sprays alternates with bouquets of daffodils, carnations and large leaves. These are separated by a pendant design in two places and by a triangular floral design in two places.

The pattern is fairly set within its lines and only a faint blurring of the blue appears on the face, but the reverse side of the dish is also faintly blue.

This pattern may be borderline.

English, marked as above, Mk. 2648, L.V., c. 1900

NONPAREIL

Made by J. & G. Meakin

The cream pitcher photographed is blue edged, scalloped and is embossed with scrolls around the top and on the body. Small sprays of bachelor buttons are placed casually around the body.

This pattern is very similar to "Messina" and "Clifton" by Alfred Meakin.

English, marked as above, Mk. 2602, L.V., c. 1907

OAKLAND

Made by John Maddock

Square sauce dishes and ice cream dishes were a novelty in the late Victorian times. This example is scalloped and is gilt edged.

The floral design is of dogwood blossoms and large leaves.

This dish is not deeply flown and may be borderline.

English, marked as above, Mk. 2463, L.V., c. 1895

ORCHID

Made by John Maddock & Sons, Ltd.

The spout and handle of this teapot are covered with dark blue embellished with gold. The main design on the body is of large orchid blooms and thin reed-like leaves. Gold lustre has been placed over a leafy pattern in the background.

The pie plate photographed is printed with an asymetrical pattern consisting of one large orchid and leaves, with sprays of smaller flowers placed opposite a small butterfly orchid, and also opposite a trio of small buds.

English, marked as above, Mk. 2464, L.V., c. 1896

PANSIES

Made by Empire Porcelain Co.

The edge of this cake plate is scalloped and heavily embossed with scroll and wave forms. Dark cobalt has been placed over this and fades toward the center.

A coloured decal of pansies and leaves in tones of orange, lemon and pale green has been placed in the center.

Gold lustre also decorates the fancy edge.

English, marked as above, Mk. 1488, L.V., c. 1896

PANSIES

Made by Sebring Pottery

The entire body of this four handled cake plate is flown with a blue that has a lavender cast. The edge is heavily embossed with scrolls, flowers and large ovals. Gold lustre has been placed around the edges.

The design of pansies covers the well.

American, marked as above, Mk. 3 (pg. 147, Thorn), L.V., c. 1887

PANSY

Made by Johnson Bros.

The rim of this pitcher is scalloped and outlined in white. The top part of the body is embossed with oval beaded medallions and scrolls over a cobalt field. The main design consists of pansies, leaves and buds.

English, marked as above, Mk. 2177, L. V., c. 1905

150

PARIS

Made by Johnson Bros.

The saucer photographed is printed in a greyish blue. It is irregularly scalloped and the pattern is asymetrical.

A large spray of poppies is placed on one side of the dish and smaller bouquets are placed at two other spots around the rim.

English, marked as above, Mk. 2177, L.V., c. 1900

PASSION FLOWER

Made by Minton

The raised outer edge of this scalloped plate is printed with stems and leaves.

The entire rim is printed with large exotic passion flowers and leaves and tendrils. A single blossom of the same species is placed in the center of the well. The passion flower is a vigorous, climbing plant with showy starlike 2-1/2 inch flowers. It is greenish white and its tall corona is composed of filaments which are blue at the top, white in the middle and purplish at the base.

The exact mark is shown on plate five of Godden's book.

English, marked M. & Co., Mk. 2694, dated Nov. 1846, E.V., c. 1846

PEARL

Made by Upper Hanley Potteries

The saucer photographed is scalloped and gilt edged. The pattern is printed in slate blue and consists of a somewhat formalized hibiscus, buds and leaves that are placed to swirl around the rim. This may be border-line.

English, marked as above, Mk. 3928, Registry #421239, L.V., c. 1904

PEONY
Made by Ridgways

This pattern is pictured on a large wash basin. It is scalloped and embossed around the edge. Two groups of large realistic peonies and leaves are placed on two facing sides of the inner surface. There are scattered single blossoms on the outer surface. *(not shown.)*

English, marked as above, Mk. 3313 L.V., c. 1910.

PERTH
Made by W. H. Grindley

The pitcher shown is deeply scalloped around the throat and again at the pedestal. The edges are gilded and beaded. The body of the vessel is divided by a wide band of small flowers, foliated scrolls and this is also scalloped and beaded. The floral design is of wild roses, daisies and large leaves.

English, marked as above, Mk. 1842, L.V., c. 1891.

POPPEA

Made by Grimwade Ltd.

This basin is decorated with a very large design of poppies, leaves and stems both on the outside and within the bowl.

The upper edge is trimmed with a dark band on which poppies alternate with foliated scrolls.

English, marked as above, Mk. 1827, L.V., c. 1906

POPPIES

Made by The Sebring Co.

This celery dish is scalloped, fluted and has pierced handles. The dark edge is covered with lustre. The entire dish is blue that fades from edge to center.

Two large poppies are placed lengthwise across the well.

No pattern name is given. We will use this name to catalogue. The backstamp is marked porcelain, but the dish is earthenware.

American, See Thorn (pg. 147, Mk. 3), L.V., c. 1887

POPPY

Made by Johnson Bros.

The baroque handle on this water pitcher is gilded and printed with blue scrolls.

The top is scalloped and the collar is printed with small flowers and scrolls contained within a heavy row of bead embossing.

The top of the body is slanted and then a deep indentation separates the top from the main part of the vessel. Large poppies are printed on this section.

The pedestal base has a scalloped foot.

English, marked as above, Mark 2177 L.V., c. 1900

PRINCE

Made by Wood & Sons

This squat little pitcher is scalloped and shell embossed and its collar is trimmed with a narrow band of diamond diapering. Scrolls are placed around the base.

The design on the body is the same on both sides and consists of a bouquet of anemones, leaves and sprigs.

English, marked as above, Mk. 4285, L.V., c. 1900

PRINCESS

Made by Wood & Sons

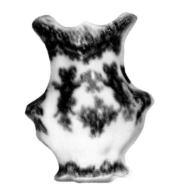

This is a toothbrush holder and the top edge is scalloped and edged with a diamond diaper pattern contained within floral scrolls. The collar is heavily embossed with shell and wave forms. The diamond design is placed around the pedestal which is also indented and trimmed with shell embossing.

The design on the body is composed of rococo reserves trimmed at the top with bowknots and enclosing a leaf form alternating with floral pendants. A shell form is placed between these to form an arch and a small bouquet of wild roses is placed within the reserves formed by the arches.

English, marked as above, Mk. 4285, L.V., c. 1900

RICHMOND

Made by W. H. Grindley

The plate photographed is scalloped, embossed with shells and scrolls and is gilt edged. The design appears on the rim and consists of small flowers, stems and leaves, which are placed over the embossed shell forms.

English, marked as above, Mk. 1842, L.V., c. 1891

RINCEAUX
Made by Villeroy & Boch

This little gilt edged dish is scalloped. The border is printed in a medium dark blue and a lighter shade of greyish blue. The design on the rim consists of six scrolled reserves, three of these contain wild roses and alternate with three containing cultivated roses. The well is encircled with a large spear point wreath. The central bouquet consists of a large wild rose surrounded by other small flowers, leaves and sprigs.

The word "Rinceaux" means a scroll pattern or ornament.

German, marked V & B, See Thorn (Mk. 43, Pg. 37).

ROSE
Made by Bourne & Leigh

Two shades of blue are used to print the design on this toothbrush holder. The collar is decorated with a dark cobalt and also a slate blue in a pattern of foliated scrolls.

The design on the body is composed of a pair of roses, both large and full blown and one rose in side view with long stems and luxurious leaves.

English, marked E.V. & J.E.L., like Mk. 486, L.V., c. 1910

ROSE

Made by Keeling & Co.

The item photographed is a stand for a teapot. Large roses are printed on it and stalks of larkspur are placed in the background. There is much gold paint around the roses and gold lustre has been placed around the edge.

English, marked K & Co. B, Mk. 2243, L.V., c. 1886

ROSE

Made by Ridgways

The bowl photographed is scalloped and is dark edged and embossed with small scrolls and flowers and fleur-de-lis. The pattern appears on the rim only and consists of six groups of roses in full bloom. These are separated by scrolled triangular cartouches on the upper part of the rim. The well is encircled by a design of scrolls that form cyma curves and arches.

The second photograph shows a pickle dish in the same pattern.

Also, this pattern has been observed printed in a greenish grey blue.

English, marked as above, Mk. 3312, L.V., c. 1910

ROSE AND IVY

Made by Brown-Westhead, Moore & Co.

The scalloped plate photographed is embossed with a single deep line around the outer edge.

The pattern consists principally of large ivy leaves that surround the rim. A pair of rose buds on a long thorned stem is placed at one side and enters the well. The well itself is circled by blue lines that pass through three rolled scrolls and then terminate in a leaf design that resembles a mask.

English, marked as above, Registry date September 23, 1870, Mk. 679, M.V., c. 1870.

ROSE AND JESSAMINE

Made by Josiah Wedgwood

The rim of this dish is unevenly scalloped and is printed with heavy scrolls.

The large central design covers the entire well and the sides of the dish and consists of long-stemmed roses with many leaves and buds. A sprig of star shaped flowers, jessamine, (jasmine) are placed near the bottom of the design.

English, marked as above, Mk. 4085, M.V., c. 1850

ROSEDALE

Made by Furnivals Ltd.

This scalloped plate is decorated on the rim with a wreath composed of single ruffled peony-type flowers with stems and leaves placed toward the right to form a swirling effect. The tips of the leaves appears on the slope of the well.

English, marked as above, Mk. 1652, Registry #339344, L.V., c. 1891

157

ROSERIE
Made by Dunn Bennett & Co.

This gently scalloped soup plate has a gilded edge and is embossed with small scrolls. The design around the upper rim forms a wreath of small rose leaves. The rest of the border is covered with single small roses, and sprigs from these descend into the well.

The plate is printed in green and blue and the design details are decorated with gold.

English, marked as above, Mk. 1422, L.V., c. 1900

ROWENA
Made by Fleming

The platter at hand is unevenly scalloped and has an irregular oval outline. The edge is detailed with scroll embossing and gold lustre has been sprayed over an outer blue border.

The dish is covered with five large groups of various flowers, roses, pansies and nasturtiums set in small blue fields.

Scottish, marked as above, Mk. 972, L.V., c. 1900

ST. LOUIS
Made by Johnson Bros.

The edge of this plate is scalloped and is encircled with bead and scallop embossing. The upper border is printed in a soft dark blue. Superimposed on this in three pieces is a dark transfer printing of peach blossoms and boughs. These extend over the lower half of the rim and enter the well at three spots.

English, marked as above, like Mk. 2177, L.V., c. 1900

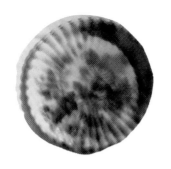

SASKIA
Maker Unknown

The fluted mold used for this cake plate is unusual and is its most striking design element.

The pattern covers most of the area and consists of large chrysanthemums, buds and leaves. A coppery gold lustre appears around the outer edge.

English, marked only England, L.V., c. 1891

SEVRES
Made by Wood & Sons

This plate is scalloped, beaded and embossed, Asters are printed around the rim, and a wreath of forget-me-nots encircles the well. Gold filigree has been placed on the large flowers and leaves.

English, marked as above, Mk. 4288, Registry #412432, (Also can be found marked NWP (New Wharf Pottery) which was absorbed by Wood & Sons in 1894), L.V., c. 1900

SHARON
Maker Unknown

The Kentucky lady who brought this pitcher, with its basin, to be photographed bears the above name and since there is no mark on either piece of her set, we will use this name to catalogue the pattern.

The mold used was very elaborate and produced a heavily embossed design of scrolls and shells which jut out from the body. Heavy blue has been placed over these elements. The handle is fragile in comparison to the ornate body.

The pattern consists of large daffodils, leaves and sprigs set within the panels created by the embossing.

Probably English, probably M.V.

SIBYL

Made by Wedgwood & Co. Ltd.

The pattern of large poppies is placed around the rim of this scalloped, beaded and scroll embossed saucer. One poppy is placed in its center.

English, marked as above, Mk. 4059, L.V., c. 1906

SOLA

Made by William Alsagar Adderly

In this picture we see the drainer from a sponge dish. On it is pictured the five-petalled flowers and the leaves of a form of tomato plant, Solanaceae. Gold has been placed on the pattern in order to accent the details.

English, marked W.A.A., Mk. 49, L.V., c. 1880

SOMERSET

Made by W. H. Grindley

This gilt edged scalloped platter is embossed with scrolls and shells. The pattern appears on the rim and consists of swags of small flowers and sprigs that are linked by dark leaf forms.

The backstamp on the piece differs from the familiar Grindley globe mark (1842). This mark is found as well as the next mark which is a green wreath (1843) so it is difficult to date. L.V., c. 1910

160

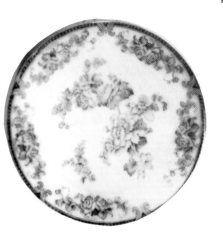

SPANISH ROSE
Made by Davenport

The border of this plate is edged with a band of lozenge design with pairs of foliated scrolls dividing the rim into five sections. In each there is printed two roses with leaves.

The center is printed with an asymetrical sprawling design of large roses and leaves and one small spray of wild roses.

English, marked as above, dated (impressed), Mk. 1181, M.V., c. 1862

SUMMERTIME
Made by Edge Malkin & Co.

Only the rim of this unevenly scalloped plate bears a pattern. The outer edge is marked with a narrow rope design and small groups of anemones and sprigs form a continuous wreath around the dish.

English, marked as above, Mk. 1445, L.V., c. 1900

SUNFLOWER
Made by W. T. Copeland

Red and yellow were used over the glaze to accent the flowers on this small tureen. The printing is in deep cobalt. The rim design around the lid consists of foliated large scrolls. The flower pattern is placed on the body and is composed of a round bouquet, somewhat in the oriental style, which is centered by a large sunflower. The handles are applied with large oak leaves and acorns.

There is no pattern name on the piece. This name is used to catalogue the design until the correct name is ascertained.

English, marked Copeland, Late Spode, Mk. 1068, E.V., c. 1853

SWALLOW
Made by Wedgwood

This plate is gently scalloped and its outer edge is detailed with a band that is encircled by coiled rings.

The pattern of leaves and blossoms covers the entire plate and a swallow is depicted on the rim.

English, marked as above, dated, stamped March 1900, See Godden (pg. 658), L.V., c. 1900

SWEETBRIER
Made by Burgess & Leigh

This jar is embossed with large fleur-de-lis. Both the top and bottom of the vessel are decorated with dark cobalt.

The pattern is scattered over the surface, and consists of the flowers and leaves of sweetbrier, a form of rose, Rosa Eglantine, found in Europe and central Asia. It has a tall stem, hooked prickles and bristles and a single pink flower.

English, marked B. & L., Mk. 712, M. V., c. 1862.

TINE
Made by Stanley Pottery Co.

This saucer is printed with exactly the same pattern as "Touraine" and carries the same registry number as the "Touraine" made by Henry Alcock and the Stanley Pottery Company. Since the pattern name is in italics it would be a logical guess that this name was a nickname or a shortening of "Touraine."

English, marked as above, Registry #329815, L.V., c. 1898

TOGO
Made by Hollinshead & Kirkham

This is a picture of the lid that is part of a covered vegetable dish. It is octagonal in shape and also gently scalloped.

The outer edge is decorated with a narrow band of criss cross trellis and small slanted lines. The rim design consists of trailing clumps of roses, stems and leaves that alternate with six petalled flowers placed in front of large round lily pads.

English, marked as above, Mk. 2073, L.V., c. 1900

TULIP
Made by Johnson Bros.

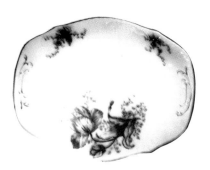

This flower is printed in a soft light blue. A large open tulip and a closed bud with their large pointed leaves are placed at one side of this small platter. Small sprays are placed around the leaves and flowers and two other sprays are placed at the opposite side of the dish.

English, marked as above, Registry #208691, Mk. 2177, L.V., c. 1900

TULIPS
Maker Unknown

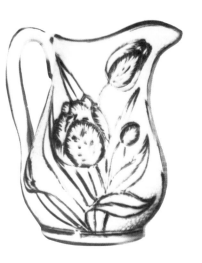

A unique method has been used to make this pitcher. The entire background is raised with a small seed pattern.

The bold design of tulips and leaves is so thick that it gives a three dimensional effect. Cobalt and gold lustre have been placed over the flowers and the blue has been allowed to flow on the floral design. The same treatment has been used around the plain top and lip and also on the base. The handle is embossed with a single oval and carries a single stripe of blue and gold.

Probably English, probably M.V.

VELARIAN
Made by Samuel Alcock & Co.

This name is probably a misspelling for the word Valerian, a plant that has numerous small blossoms on long stalks which bear shaggy leaves.

The printing is in slate blue and the dish is unevenly scalloped and the open leafy handles are deeply embossed. There is also an embossed edging band around the outer rim, which is divided into four large panels containing dahlias and four smaller panels containing valerian. The panels are constructed of flowering leafy branches and these surround the well.

The central bouquet contains striped ribbon grass, jonquils, a large lily and some sprigs.

English, marked as above, marked with a beehive mark, Like Mk. 77, E.V., c. 1845

VENICE
Maker Unknown

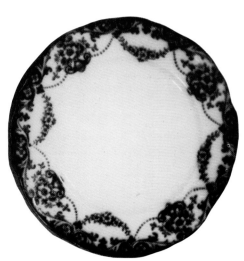

This plate is unevenly scalloped and the design appears only on the rim. The outer edge is wreathed with foliated scrolls that contain pairs of stylized flowers with four petals.

There are eight reserves formed at the top and garlands and beading link the bottom of the design and in four of these are urns with scrolled handles that contain bouquets of wild roses.

English, Registry #541031, L.V., c. 1908

VICTOR
Made by Thomas Booth & Co.

The pitcher photographed is scalloped at its top edge and base. It is embossed with scrolls and the under lip is also embossed. The body of the vessel is divided into sections by embossed vertical panels which are outlined with gold. Wild roses and leaves are printed in the spaces between the panels.

English, marked T.B.&Co. T, Mk. 47, M.V., c. 1872

164

VIOLETS
Maker Unknown

This plate is scalloped and gilt edged. The rim is fluted. The design is asymetrical. One large group of flowers is flanked by trailing violets and stems which enter the well. A smaller floral group is placed on the opposite rim.

There is no backstamp on this plate. The name is used to catalogue the pattern.

Probably English, probably L. V.

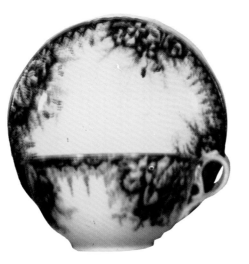

VIOLETTE
Made by Keller & Guerin

This dish is printed in a dark greyish blue. Three groups of violets, leaves and sprays are separated around the rim by a gothic design of tre-foil arches from which a design of crossed lines and beads trail toward the center of the plate.

French, marked K. & G., Luneville, See Thorn (page 7, Mk. 2), L.V. c. 1891

WARWICK
Made by Johnson Bros.

This plate is deeply scalloped and a line of double scallops is embossed within the edge.

The sprawling pattern of large leaves and gooseberries is placed asymetrically, that is predominantly on one side, and covers part of the well.

English, marked as above, Mk. 2177, L.V., c. 1900

WARWICK PANSY

Made by Warwick China Co.

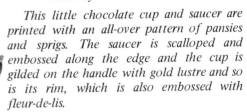

This little chocolate cup and saucer are printed with an all-over pattern of pansies and sprigs. The saucer is scalloped and embossed along the edge and the cup is gilded on the handle with gold lustre and so is its rim, which is also embossed with fleur-de-lis.

American, marked as above, See Thorn (pg. 152, Mk. 38), L.V., c. 1900

WATER NYMPH

Made by Josiah Wedgwood

The chop plate photographed is unevenly scalloped and is embossed with a border band interspersed with foliated scrolls over a similar printed edging.

The floral design which covers the well and extends up onto the rim consists of large water lilies and leaves. The botanical name for water lily is "nymphae".

English, marked as above, dated 1872, Mk. 4074, M.V., c. 1872

WILD ROSE

Made by Wm. Adams & Co.

This cereal bowl is printed in a greyish blue and in black. Its edge is slightly scalloped and deep scroll and shell like embossing are placed around the rim, which is printed with roses, three leaf clovers and very dark leaves on a net background.

The central design is of two large roses and buds, black leaves and leafy foliage.

English, marked as above, like Mk. 29, L.V., c. 1900

166

WINDSOR WREATH
Made by Wood & Brownfield

The wreath which gives this plate its name appears on both the rim and well and consists of at least eight different stylized flowers and leaves. Small sprigs and buds are also added to the design.

The border is like that of "Ambrosia" and consists of embossed edging interrupted at five points with pairs of foliated scrolls, which have been coloured with cobalt.

English, marked W. & B., Mk. 4242, E.V., c. 1845

WOODLAND
Made by Wood & Sons

This gently scalloped plate has wave-like embossing that is detailed with gold trim. The outer edge has a scrolled border of vertical lines. Below this on the rim is a thick wreath of small flowers from which sprigs extend toward the center. The well is outlined by scrolled swags and tiny garlands.

English, marked as above, Mk. 4285, Registry #339529, L.V., c. 1891

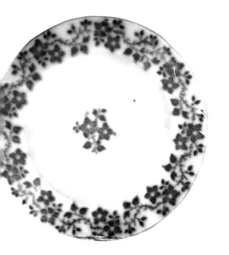

WREATH
Made by Charles Meigh

The deep dish pictured has a rim design of small five petalled flowers, thorny stems and leaves.

A pair of the flowers on a single stem and with leaves is placed in the center of the well.

No name is given on the backstamp. This name is given to catalogue.

English, marked "Imperial Stone China", Mk. 2618, E.V., c. 1842

YORK

Made by W. & E. Corn

The scalloped edge of this dish is outlined by fine lattice work enclosed in a wreath of fleur-de-lis and small arch forms. The design is asymetrical. On one side there is a large scrolled floral cartouche, with sprays of roses going into the center of the well. Two small scroll and spray designs are placed opposite the large design.

English, marked as above, Mk. 1113, L.V., c. 1900

THE FOLLOWING PATTERNS HAVE NO PICTURES AVAILABLE

CHATSWORTH

Made by George Jones & Son

This pattern appears on a dark edged late that is not scalloped and the design onsists of daisies and sprays placed around he rim, part of which enters the well.

English, Registered in 1884, marked as bove, Mk. 2218, L.V., c. 1891

DOREEN

Made by W. H. Grindley

This pattern consists of large floral sprays s observed on a vessel at an antique show. he flowers were placed asymetrically.

English, marked as above, Mk. 1842, ..V., c. 1891

HARVEST

Made by Sampson Hancock & Son

This pattern consists of large frilly poppies grouped closely together on five stems.

English, marked as above, Mk. 1932, L.V., c. 1906

HATFIELD

Made by Ralph Hammersley & Son

A platter observed in a shop was printed in a blackish blue. A large spray of columbine was placed across one side and two smaller sprays, one of baby's breath, and one of small roses, are placed on the opposite side of the rim.

English, marked R.H. &S., Mk. 1914, L.V., c. 1886

JARDINIERE

Made by Villeroy & Bach

This pattern closely resembles "Dresden" issued by the same firm. Three large roses are placed around the rim and are connected by a lacy pattern of diamond and dots.

One large rose and bud is placed in the center. Its leaves form a swirling pattern around it.

German, marked V.R.B. in a floral cartouche, See Thorn (page 37 Mk. 43), L.V., c. 1880

PETUNIA

Made by Wiltshaw & Robinson

A bowl observed in an antique show bears the above name and was decorated with petunias and stems in a very dark cobalt.

English, marked W.&R., Carlton Ware, Mk. 4201, Registry #337779, L.V., c. 1900

STRATFORD

Made by Ridgways

This pattern is printed in a greyish blue. The outer edge of the plate is detailed with a dark band that is painted with gold.

Roses are placed asymetrically around the rim, and one is placed off center in the well.

English, marked as above, Mk. 3312, L.C., c. 1891

WALTON

Made by Ford & Sons

A wash basin and pitcher observed at an antique shop bore a pattern of large dahlias and leaves that covered most of the surfaces. The rims of both were deeply scalloped and were gilt edged.

English, marked F. & Sons. Mk. 1585, L.V., c. 1900

FLORAL CATEGORY
ADDENDA AND CORRECTIONS TO BOOK ONE

page 84   **"AMBROSIA"** *It is possible that this pattern was made by Wood and Brownfield. The molded edge has been found on plates made by this firm (Birmah for one.) If s it dates c. 1840.*

page 85   **"ANEMONE"** *This is a picture of a cake plate in this pattern and it shows that the pattern clearly contains a central floral motif.*

page 92   **"CEICEL"** *This pattern is identical to the "Meissen" pattern of F Melhem.*

page 96   **"CORA"** *The name of this pattern is probably "DORA".*

page 98   **"DOROTHY"** *This pattern may be borderline.*

page 103 **"GIRONDE"** *The word is misspelled in the last sentence of the description. Gironde is the correct spelling.*

page 107 **"IRIS"** *The maker of this pattern has been identified as Clementson Bros. The mark is 908, the pattern is English and dates L.V., c. 1905.*

page 110 **"LILY"** *Made by Johnson Bros. We have photographed a basin in this design that shows the swirling effect of the pattern when seen as a whole.*

age 111 **"LOBELIA"** *This pattern has been observed at antique shows and although some pieces do seem to be flown, it may be borderline.*

age 112 **"LORCH"** *Should read "LARCH". A larch is a coniferous tree, one of the group of trees such as pine, fir and spruce. This design is of pine needles.*

age 112 **"LORRAINE"** *This pattern may be borderline.*

age 113 **"LUZERNE"** *This pattern is identical to "WALDORF" made at first by New Wharf Pottery and then later by Wood & Sons when they purchased the New Wharf Pottery in 1894. The blank (mold) may differ but the border and the medallion center are the same. The Luzerne medallion may be larger.*

age 115 **"MEISSEN"** *The Libertas mark with the eagles may be a F. Melhem mark.*

age 119 **"MILLAIS"** *This may be a borderline pattern.*

age 119 **"MONTANA"** *This picture shows the pattern on a round dish.*

page 122 **"NORWICH"** *This is "ASHBURTON" (See Addenda note for page 136.)*

page 125 **"PEACH ROYAL"** *This pattern is correctly named "PEÀCH" but some collectors call it as above by using the word 'royal' from the backstamp which reads 'Royal Semi Porcelain'.*

page 126 **"QUEEN CHARLOTTE"** *The correct name of the pattern is "QUEEN'S BORDER".*

page 131 **"SYDNEY"** *We show a clearer picture of the pattern.*

page 133 **"VENICE"** *We show a clearer picture of the pattern.*

page 135 **"WALDORF"** *This pattern was made by Mercer in the United States (See LUZERNE) and by Wood and Sons after they purchased New Wharf Pottery in 1894*

ge 136 **"ACANTHA"** *Made by J. & G. Meakin. This is a picture of this pattern as it appears on a sauce dish which is scalloped and embossed with roses, scrolls and shells. The outer edge is printed with small scallop shells, frothy vertical lines and little rose sprigs. The well is outlined by a wreath of heart designs set in rounded triangles and small spear points. The pattern is printed in slate blue. It is English, marked as above, Mk. 2900, L.V., c. 1891.*

ge 136 **"ARGYLE"** *made by Wood & Son. We present a picture of a tureen, the body is encircled by a wreath of small flowers, and above that there are swags made of eight small round roses. Between the two designs there are small sprigs.*

This design is repeated on the lid with the wreath placed toward the top and the swags placed around the edge. Gold has been placed on the swags on the lid.

page 136 **"ASHBURTON"** *Made by W. H. Grindley. This plate is scalloped and is embossed with beading and small flowers. The design consists of large fern-like plants, the tip of which enter the well. These are separated by small single roses and leaves .*

English, marked as above, Mk. 1842, L.V. c. 1891.

page 136 **"ASTORIA"** *Made by Johnson Bros. The edge of this plate is scalloped and embossed with scrolls and tiny round berries with leaves. The lower edge of the rim is indented with scallops. The upper border design consists of large very dark leaf forms that alternate with small scrolled cartouches that enclose netting. Sprigs of daisies are placed around the lower part of the rim, and the well is encircled with a wreath of dark small leaves and scrolls.*

English, Marked as above, Mk. 2177, L.V., c. 1900.

ge 137 **"BRUSSELS"** *We show a photograph of a platter that illustrates the fish scale embossing around the edge, and the placing of the floral groups of lilies that alternate with the triangular fleur-de-lis designs.*

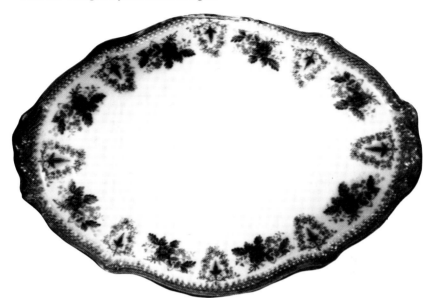

ge 137 **"BUTE"** *This pattern is not correctly catalogued, it should be considered miscellaneous as it combines elements of Art Nouveau, and Baroque Art. It therefore is catalogued in Book II in the Miscellaneous Category.*

ge 137 **"CAMPION"** *Should read "made by W. H. Grindley".*

ge 137 **"DEL MONTE"** *This is a photograph of a plate in the pattern and shows the design of jonquils and sprigs connected by elongated ribbon-like stems.*

page 137 **"DORA"** *See correction of plate listed as "CORA".*

page 138 **"GLOIRE DE DIJON"** *Here are two pictures of items in this pattern. The pitcher printed in a silvery light blue. Its collar is a clear pale blue and the top edge is banded in gold. A simple blue band separates the collar and body. The soap dish and i drainer are printed with the rose design in a very dark cobalt. Therefore, Doulto made merchandise in the pattern in at least these two colour variations.*

page 138 **"NAVY"** *The plate photographed is scalloped and gilt edged. The design appear only on the rim and consists of thickly bunched bouquets of small flowers and sprigs Around the outer edge there are six small triangular spaces filled with shaded lines Some gold has been placed in curliques over the border. The backstamp is interesting in that it consists of the usual Till globe mark with star, but this is surmounted by battleship. One could conjecture that this pattern was indeed made for the Britis Navy.*

ge 138 **"NORBERRY"** *Should read "Norbury". We show a picture of the top of a sponge dish. Mk. 1333.*

ge 139 **"PLYMOUTH"** *Made by New Wharf Pottery. This platter is scalloped and embossed with ribbons and scrolls around the upper rim. The embossing stands out over a scrolled border that contains small flowers. Groups of roses, both cultivated and wild are placed around the deep rim. A dark blue band, printed with a wreath of small flowers and leaves, and edged at the top with a spear point design encircles the well. This printing is slate blue.*

English, Marked as above, Mk. 2886, L.V., c. 1891.

page 139 **"PRINCESS"** *Made by Booths. An all-over pattern of sprays of roses, small flowe. and vines is printed in slate blue on this scalloped plate. It is also embossed and flut with swirling lines on the rim. This pattern carries the Registry number 183183.*

page 139 **"TYNE"** *Made by Bridgwood & Sons. The platter photographed is printed in a very dark slate blue. It is unevenly scalloped and a dark band runs around the outer edge. Scrolled embossing is placed around the upper rim. The pattern is composed o sprawling wild flowers with long curving stems and large elongated leaves. The Tyne River is located in Northumberland, England.*

English, Marked as above, Mk. 2886, L.V., c. 1891.

PLATE XII

Kyber by W. Adams & Co., Collection of Leslie Holstner, Jr., Indiana

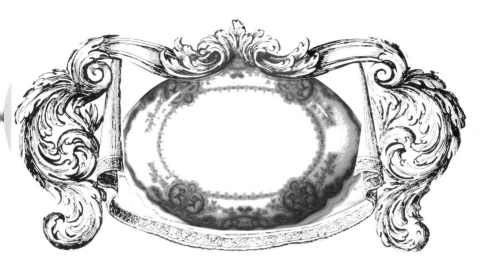

Art Nouveau Category

ALMA

Maker Unknown

The top of the pitcher photographed is gently scalloped and the collar is embossed with large scrolls that form triangular arches. The foot is also scalloped and the bottom of the body is embossed with large fleur-de-lis. Gold has been placed over some of the design. The embossed fleur-de-lis below the central part of the body of the vessel are printed in dark cobalt. The collar bears a design of inverted fans and floral forms and the embossed spout is entirely printed in blue with gold overpainted on the details.

The design on the body is floral and is composed of five large asters and leaves, but it is also baroque and contains scrolls. The bottom of the bouquet is composed of long foliated scrolls, stylized flower forms and laurel leaf wreaths on either side of the bottom of the scrolls.

English (probably), L.V., c. 1880

ALTON

Made by W. H. Grindley

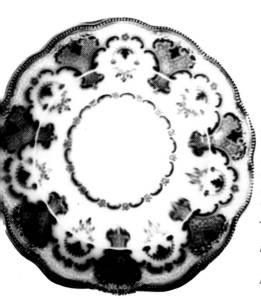

The soup plate photographed is scalloped, beaded and embossed with scrolls and treillage. The pattern on the rim enters deeply into the well and consists of arched reserves which contain a circular design of dots and small pendant sprigs. These are separated by deep spade shaped forms that contain small flowers topped by a leafy fleur-de-lis.

The center of the well is encircled by a ring of alternate scrolls and small flowers.

English, marked as above, Mark 1842, L.V., c. 1891.

ASTORIA
Made by The Empire Porcelain Co.

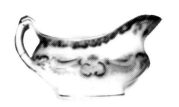

The gravy boat photographed has a border of dark scallops. The design appears on the body and consists of a central design of three little flowers under a small scrolled pediment. It is flanked by long foliated scrolls containing beading. Scallop lines are placed above the length of the pattern. Gold has been placed over parts of the design.

English, marked as above, like mark 1488, L.V., c. 1905.

ASTORIA
Made by Pitcairns Ltd.

This cream ewer is scalloped and embossed. The collar is decorated with a band of triangles and elongated ovals connected by a thick line of scrolls.

The body bears a pattern of fairly large single flowers and buds spaced equally apart around the widest section. A similar design, but smaller is placed around the pedestal base.

English, marked as above, Mark 3052, L.V., c. 1895.

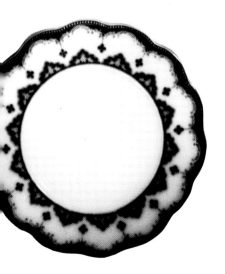

ASTRAL
Made by W. H. Grindley

The scalloped dark edge of this plate is beaded and then is embossed with small scrolls set over an arched scalloped printed line. Suspended from the outer border are small star shapes composed of 4 diamond points.

The lower part of the rim is encircled by triangular dark reserves enclosing a small stylized flower and three leaves.

English, Registry mark 426592, marked as above, Mark 1842, L.V., c. 1891.

BALTIC
Made by W. H. Grindley

This saucer is unevenly scalloped and its edge is detailed with a very dark printed scalloped band from which 6 dark petalled circles descend. These are surrounded by little stylized flowers and leaves in a lighter blue and alternate with an inverted heart design composed of fleur-de-lis.

The well is defined by a circular patterned band.

English, marked as above, Mark 1842, L.V., c. 1891.

BELL
Made by Thos. Rathbone & Co.

This plate is unevenly scalloped and there is some gold around the edge. The upper rim is decorated with a dark band and long arrow-form scrolls that are beaded on the lower edge. The pattern appears on the rim only and is divided into three sections by a shield form containing a small bell like form. The main design is of stylized bell flowers and leaves.

English, marked as above, Mark 3205, L.V., c. 1910.

BELMONT
Made by W. H. Grindley

The pitcher photographed is printed in a slate blue and navy blue.

The pattern on the body consists of a heart shaped design composed of scrolls and a foliated inner double lobe effect, surrounding a field of forget-me-nots and dots.

Garlands of small flowers are festooned from the main heart design on either side of a pendant leaf with a double scrolls.

The piece is heavily embossed at its collar and base, and around the upper edge and on the handle.

English, marked as above, Mark 1842, L.V., c. 1891.

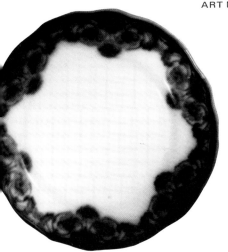

BERKLEY
Made by Wood & Sons

This unevenly scalloped, dark edged plate is embossed with a fan shape at six places on the rim.

The print appears only on the rim and consists of a trio of flowers with swirling stems that are placed to form a triangle below the fan forms. The spaces between the flower designs are filled with leaves formed like scrolls and a pair of little cup-shaped flowers.

English, marked as above, Mk. 4285, L.V., c. 1905

BEVERLY
Made by Henry Alcock & Co., Ltd.

This unevenly scalloped egg platter is printed in slate blue. The design is placed on the rim and consists of alternating patterns, the first consists of a group of three daffodils on a triangular background flanked by wings containing a scaled diaper design, and the second consists of a tongs-like design that contains a single daffodil flanked by rings containing small flowers. Both elements are linked by garlands of forget-me-nots and sprigs. The well is defined by a narrow ribbon.

English, marked as above, Mk. 65, L.V., c. 1905

BLENHEIM
Made by Sampson Hancock & Son

This plate is gilt edged and scalloped. The outer edge is decorated with a dark dotted band that is interrupted by six cartouches containing a round stylized flower and by six small spade shaped and scrolled reserves.

The rim pattern consist of stylized columbine and long swirling stems which meet at the bottom of the rim and form a wreath around the well. This is elaborated with small stylized floral designs and a geometric fleur-de-lis.

English, Registry Mark #391504, marked S. H. & Son, Mk. 1923, L.V., c. 1910.

BRENTFORD

Made by Ford & Sons Ltd.

This platter is printed in a greyish blue. The pattern appears on the rim only and consists of a trio of stylized flowers that are set on a field of vertical straight lines. In each corner there is a heart shaped design composed of scrolls which connect to the floral pattern by long foliated scrolls.

English, marked F. & Sons Ltd., Mk. 1586, L.V., c. 1910

BURNHAM

Made by Ridgways

The edge of this gently scalloped saucer is outlined by a border of small stylized round flowers and leaves contained in a narrow band.

The design appears on the rim and consists of three elongated patterns that give the effect of a wreath. They are composed of facing pairs of long swirling scrolls that circle under themselves in a whiplash effect and enclose a small stylized flower with a dark center. Small sprigs are entwined about the scrolls and extend from each end almost to the point of reaching the next design.

This name mark is hard to decipher, the first few letters look like, BURH or BURN, but the makers name is clear.

English, marked as above, Mk. 3310, L.V., c. 1885

CAMBRIDGE

Made by Hollinshead & Kirkham

This is an example of late Art Nouveau showing the trend toward Art Deco. The geometric triangular design flanks a curved Moorish form. These alternate with a fan design that consists of a large stylized five petaled flower set against a fish scale design. Small flowers, leaves and stems enter the well from the latter design element.

This is printed in a greyish blue ink.

English, marked as above, Mk. 2073, L.V., c. 1910

CLARENDON

Made by Henry Alcock & Co., Ltd.

The unevenly scalloped and dark edged rim of this platter is decorated with the stylized flower and stem forms so typical of art nouveau. Inverted heart-shaped reserves containing realistic daffodils alternate with a vase shape topped by a stylized flower and flanked by formalized daffodils. The two designs are joined at the well by whip lash scrolls.

English, marked as above, Mk. 65, L.V., c. 1900

DAVENPORT

Made by Wood & Sons

This scalloped butter pat has shell embossing at four places on the rim which is outlined with both an embossed line and a dark band. The border design consists of groups of three jonquils flanked by very dark leaves and these are joined by stem like scrolls and smaller dark leaves.

English, marked as above, Mk. 4285, L.V., c. 1907

DELFT

*Made by The Brownfields Guild
Pottery Society Ltd.*

The lip of this cup is lined with a narrow spear point border. The design on the rim is composed of realistic shaggy peony like flowers with very dark leaves. These are separated by scrolls and small leaves that give a stylized effect to the pattern. The medallion in the center of the plates is composed of the above type flowers with scrolls and very dark leaves.

English, marked as above, Registry Mark 210792, Mk. 669, L.V., c. 1895.

DENTON

Made by W. H. Grindley

This plate is evenly scalloped and has an outer edging of bell flowers. The design appears only on the rim and consists of stylized vase forms filled with three flowers and flanked by scrolls. These alternate with a conventionalized flower basket and floral sprays.

English, marked as above, Mk. 1842, L.V., c. 1891

DOVER

Made by Ford & Sons

The pitcher and basin photographed are scalloped and have heavy embossing which is gilded. The design consists of roses joined in a stylized triangular design by a twisting ribbon.

English, marked F. & Sons, Burslem, Mk. 1585, L.V., c. 1893.

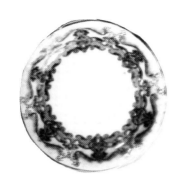

ELGAR

Made by the Upper Hanley Pottery Company

This saucer is gently and irregularly scalloped, and fleur-de-lis embossing is placed around the outer edge.

The design appears on the rim only and consists of stylized lotus forms that alternate with an inverted heart design surmounted by flowered scrolls. Both elements are joined at the bottom by a wreath, 3/4" wide, of a bluish grey color.

English, marked as above, Mk. 3298, L.V., c. 1900

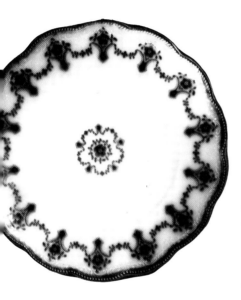

GIRTON

Made by W. H. Grindley

This plate is typical of Grindley. It is scalloped, beaded and embossed on the upper third of the rim.

The border design is composed of a series of single stylized five-petaled flowers with leaves set in a vase form. These are linked by a garland of stylized sprigs.

The center medallion consists of two concentric circles, the outer of sprig garlands and the little vase form inverted; the inner which surrounds a flower is made up entirely of sprigs.

English, marked as above, Mk. 1842, L.V., c. 1891.

HAARLEM

Made by Burgess & Leigh

The pattern on this tureen covers most of the surface. It is a stylized floral and scroll design placed in five distinct semi circular areas. The flowers are placed on leaved stems that have little berry clusters at the root ends that point toward the center. The border design is of stylized triangles and a half flower.

English, Registry Mark 457960, marked as above, Mk. 717, L.V., c. 1906.

HARTINGTON
Made by W. H. Grindley

This plate is edged with a band of beading and the rim pattern is composed of scrolls and stylized flowers with a background of diamond diaper pattern enclosed within the scrolls.

The central design is a stylized bouquet with roses, dahlias and sprigs.

English, marked as above, Mk. 1842, L.V., c. 1891

HAWKSLEY
Made by Sampson Hancock & Son

This is the scalloped top of a tureen. The design appears on the rim and consists of four heart shaped patterns that have wing like extensions at the top. These alternate with four groups of sprawling stylized sunflowers with the typical swirling stems of the Art Nouveau period.

The embossed top of this tureen and presumably the well of the plate, is encircled by a brocaded band which is interrupted at eight points under the main designs by small spear point motifs.

English, marked SH&S, Registry Mark 411972, Mk. 1933, L.V., c. 1910

HILTON
Made by Poutney & Company

This scalloped platter is beaded and embossed with little scrolls. The edge is detailed with a dark scrolled border.

The rim is divided into four sections by vertical scrolled reserves that contain small bouquets of roses. The large spaces between the reserves are decorated with a design of a large full blown rose flanked by sprays of forget-me-nots and sprigs. The lower parts of both designs are joined and form a wreath around the upper part of the well.

English, marked as above and impressed Bristol, Mk. 3107, L.V., c. 1884

HONITON

Possibly Made by Burroughs & Mountford

The edge of this plate is beaded and is outlined with a dark band that forms scallops around the upper rim. Set in each of the arches formed by the edge design is a small stylized flower. These are flanked by little round scrolls and are linked at the bottom by swags from which small chains of beads descend toward the well. Under each flower there is a deep triangular shaped garland that is the same length as the beading.

American, marked with a rampant lion and the words "Dura-Ware." Burgess · & Cambell also used this mark, but Thorn, on page 120, Mk. 28 uses the word "Honiton" as a pattern of the above firm. L.V.c. 1880

IRENE

Made by Wedgwood & Co.

This plate is unevenly scalloped and its rim is covered with a stylized design of chrysanthemum forms interposed between large foliated C curves that terminate in a three petaled iris design. These are printed on a dark background in five places and alternate with reserves that were left white and in which are printed a smaller stylized chrysanthemum.

The well is defined by a row of lacy small scrolls and a pendant design that forms a spear point circle.

English, marked as above, Mk. 4057, L.V., c. 1891

IRIS

Made by Myott, Son & Co.

This photograph of the pattern is made from the lid of a covered dish. It is typical Art Nouveau with swirling elongated stems that form patterns that surround stylized iris. The edge of the dish is slightly scalloped and it is also beaded.

English, marked as above, Mk. 2811, L.V., c. 1907

JEWEL
Made by Johnson Bros.

The pie plate photographed is scalloped and the gilt edge is further detailed with a row of small embossed scallops. The design appears only on the rim. Five pendants separate five scrolled and stylized lily designs. These two elements are joined by long cyma curves.

English, marked as above, Mk. 2177, L.V., c. 1900

KELMSCOTT
Maker Unknown

This platter is decorated in a greyish blue ink and the pattern appears only on the rim. The design consists of four large water lilies at each side of the dish. Between them there are cup shaped designs and the interspace is filled with water lily buds and the typical swirling long stems found in Art Nouveau design.

English, L.V., c. 1900

KENT
Made by Doulton Company

This pitcher is decorated with a dark blue collar on which are printed pale blue ruffled peony type large flowers. The collar is contained by foliated scrolls and groups of three poppies.

The bottom edge is trimmed with swirling scrolls and the same groupings as above.

English, marked as above, Mk. 1333, L.V., c. 1902

LICHFIELD

Made by Arthur J. Wilkinson Company

The lip and rim of this cream pitcher are bordered in blue and embossed and gilded.

The design is of a spade shape alternating with an upright leaf shaped pattern. These are linked with garlands of beading.

English, marked Royal Staffordshire Pottery, Mk. 4171, L.V., c. 1910

LUSITANIA

Made by Wood & Son

The outer rim of this dish is covered with an edging of diamond diapering contained within scrolls. Four pairs of stylized wild roses, placed on top of a scroll and leaf and flanked by foliated scrolls, are placed at equal distance around the rim.

The central pinwheel type medallion is composed of spokes of roses and scrolls radiating from a central rose.

English, marked as above, Mk. 4285, L.V., c. 1891

MONTROSE

Made by Wedgwood & Co., Ltd.

The edge of this unevenly scalloped platter is outlined with a dark cobalt band. The design appears on the rim and consists of four large trailing groups of anemones and leaves that are placed on each side of the dish. These large groups, which invade the well are joined by foliated scrolls, leaves and small flowers.

English, marked as above, Mk. 4057, L.V. c. 1900

NATAL

Made by Hollinshead & Kirkham

This plate is embossed in an unusual style with six large scallop reserves that encircle the upper half of the rim. The unevenly scalloped edge of the plate is gilded. The design appears only on the rim and consists of triangular shapes flanked by floral branches alternating with pendant basket shapes flanked by loops. These are separated by a small scroll and floral design.

Natal is a small city in Brazil that was founded in 1599.

English, marked as above, Mk. 2073, L. V., c. 1905

NEWLYN

Made by Burgess & Leigh

The ladle pictured is printed in a greyish blue and has a small scallop and triangle design around the inner edge of the bowl. The rim is trimmed in gold.

English, marked as above, Registry Mk. 640182, L. V., c. 1910

OSBORNE

Made by Till & Sons

This platter is irregularly scalloped and its edge is outlined with a dark band contained within a serrated trim. The pattern appears on the rim and consists of four large cartouches formed by leaves and foliated scrolls and containing stylized bouquets of daisy like flowers and lily of the valley sprays. These are joined by stemmed flowers and by circular medallions outlined by lily of the valley.

The well is defined by a row of iron lace pattern.

English, marked as above, Mk. 3858, L. V., c. 1891

OXFORD

Made by Johnson Bros.

The edge of this plate is scalloped and is embossed with a baroque scroll border that is printed with blue and is gilded.

The design contains small pairs of stylized flowers with leaves and scrolled stems. These alternate with a design of a pair of short plumes between which there is a heart surmounted by a dot. This design is based upon stems and leaves. A continuous band runs through the center of both elements and dips beneath the smaller design and forms a diamond.

In the center of the well there is a wreath composed of the larger rim design.

English, marked as above, like Mk. 2177, L. V., c. 1900

PERSIA

Made by Bishop and Stonier

This tureen is decorated only with very dark bands that are set upon a diaper base of small fish scale type. There are scrolls, geometric maze like lines, and Moorish cartouches and circles all set within the bands which encircle the edge of the lid and the top collar of the body.

English, marked as above, and marked 'Bisto' Mk. 386, L.V., c. 1910

POPPY

Made by W. Adams & Co.

This scalloped bowl is printed boldly with a pattern of five poppy buds linked by swirling stems on the border. A dark ring frames both upper and lower edges of the rim design.

The main design covers the well and is a highly stylized version of poppies and leaves. The most striking part of the design are the three straight stems drawn right across the dish. Two end in twin buds, the other is topped by a round flower.

This pattern was registered on January 21, 1881. The plate bears no name. We use this name to catalogue it.

English, marked as above, Mk. 29, L.V., c. 1900.

REGAL

Made by J & G Meakin

This mitten shaped relish dish is edged with dot and cross embossing. It is also embossed with small swags.

The design appears only on the rim and consists of diamond shaped cartouches that alternates with a double curve design from which a pair of hooked scrolls descend. A pale background of scrolls and sprigs fills in the background.

English, marked as above, Registered # 33287, Patented October, 1900, Mk. 2601, L.V., c. 1900

RENOWN

Made by Arthur Wilkinson Co.

Stylized water lilies are printed in greyish blue on the rim of this plate. They are set in reserves formed by flowing foliated swirls and long stems. Swags of roses are placed over the rim design. The outer edge is encircled with a twisted ribbon border and small round floral forms. Gold has been placed around the outer circular edge and over the long swirling stems.

English, marked Royal Staffordshire Pottery, Mk. 4170, L.V., c. 1907

ROSLIN

Made by Allertons

The soup plate photographed is unevenly scalloped, and the outer edge is decorated with a pattern of straight lines contained by printed arch form scallops. The printing is in a very dark greyish blue and appears only on the rim. The design consists of formalized trios of flowers and leaves that alternate with very dark cartouch forms that contain a flame like leaf design. These elements are joined by large scrolls.

English, marked as above, Mk. 88, L.V., c. 1905.

SENATOR

Made by J. Dimmock

The gravy boat photographed is scalloped, embossed and gilt trimmed. The top border consists of a band of narrow vertical lines on which are placed rounded triangular forms.

The design on the body is a stylized chrysanthemum with scrolled branches and dark leaves.

This is the same design as "Royal Blue" and "Balmoral" by Burgess and Campbell and "Floral" by Hughes.

English, marked "Cliff", Mk. 1295, L.V., c. 1900

TANKARD

Maker Unknown

This can shaped cup has an applied square angled handle with quatrefoils printed on it.

The top rim is encircled by arabesque triangles and arch forms.

The main design on the body is of a stylized lily. Small vertical sprigs adorn the base.

There are no marks of any kind on this vessel.

TOKIO

Made by Johnson Bros.

The rim of the sugar bowl photographed is scalloped and embossed, and so is its pedestal.

The design is paisley like and consists of a deep band of scrolls, dotted lines and stylized flowers and stems.

English, marked as above, Like Mk. 2177 L.V., c. 1891.

TRENT

Made by Bishop & Stonier

Much gold appears on the scallops at the top of this pitcher.

Some gold outlines the design at the bottom which is heavily embossed with scrolls and large fleur-de-lis.

The pattern on the body is very typically Art Nouveau. It consists of swirling lines that form rounded leaf shapes, a stylized large floral design and elongated stems that form an inverted heart. The collar is completely covered with a design of scrolls and stylized flowers.

English, marked B & S, Mk. 384, L.V., c. 1905

TRIESTE (THE)

Made by Johnson Bros

This plate may date after 1910. It had been mentioned (years ago) as a desirable pattern by a reliable dealer and resulted in a long search, so it will be included.

The design appears on the rim only and consists of a brocade type band of scrolls, diamonds, spades and hearts in two tones of blue.

The well is outlined by a small spear point design.

English, marked as above, Mk. 2179, L.V., c. 1910

WALBECK

Made by Sampson Hancock & Sons

This scalloped platter is edged with a dark border of printed small wave forms. On the rim there are four cartouches composed of swirling scrolls which contain stylized sunflowers. These are separated by a flowered field that contains pairs of large violets with whip lash stems.

English, marked, S.H. & S., Mk. 1933, L.V., c. 1905.

WAVERLY

Made by W. H. Grindley

This scalloped, beaded, embossed and gilt edged plate is printed with a mixture of styles. Five heart shaped foliated cartouches alternate with five little realistic bouquets, which are placed under a stylized fleur-de-lis and two bell flowers. These very different elements are held together by swags of sprigs and tiny flowers, which are placed around the outer part of the well.

English, marked as above, Mk. 1842, L.V., c. 1891.

WELBECK

Made by J. H. Weatherby & Sons, Ltd.

The scallops on this plate are gilded. The design is printed in a very dark slate blue on an almost black ground, and it is Persian on effect. Three large pointed arches enclose stylized and baroque renditions of carnations that are placed above foliated scrolls and hearts flanked with small stylized flowers and stems. These main elements are separated on the rim with inverted triangular forms filled with fish scale diapering, and flanked by swirling small flowers and stems. Foliated scrolls join the lower part of the design and a necklace of small beads threads around the well and through the middle of the design.

English, marked J.W.H. & Sons, and 'Durability', Mk. 4044, Registry number 461702, L.V. c. 1905.

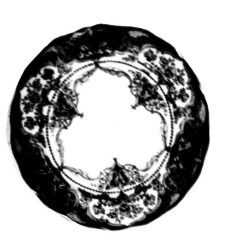

ART NOUVEAU CATEGORY
ADDENDA AND CORRECTIONS TO BOOK I

page 156 **"OREGON"** *The plate photographed shows the design more clearly than the individual vegetable dish illustrated in the first book. The white edge is scalloped and beaded. The cobalt design appears on the rim against a blackish blue background and consists of five groups of flowers. These are composed of a central four petalle round blossom flanked by inverted buds and scroll-like leaves. The stem of the forms and some leaves enter the well which is encircled by a band of embosse fleur-de-lis. Gold has been painted over the flowers.*

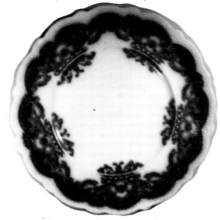

page 160 **"REGENT"** *A cup and saucer have been located that are marked "England" and which also carry a blurred backstamp that may be that of George Mountford M 2796 L.V. c. 1895*

page 160 **"REGOUTS FLOWER"** *This pattern should be placed in the categroy of Brush Stroke painted items.*

page 161 **"ROSEVILLE"** *This pattern was also made in England by Thomas Hughes.*

page 161 **"ROYSTON"** *This is a photograph of the pattern.*

ge 162 **"SEVILLE"** *This pattern was also marked "Wood & Sons" who aquired the New Wharf Pottery Co. in 1894*

ge 165 **"ATHENS"**, *made by Grimwades, Ltd. The pattern on the platter shown is placed on the rim, and consists of a pair of long sweeping wave-like scrolls centered with a shield design that is flanked by heart shaped leaves. This pattern is placed on the long sides of the dish and gives the appearance of a pair of scrolled wings, the bottom of which enter the well. The ends of the platter are decorated with a small scrolled pendant design. The two pattern elements are joined on the outer edge by a dark wavy line composed partially of the heart shaped leaves.*

English, marked Stoke Pottery, Mk. 1824, L. V. c. 1900

age 165 **"CANDIA"** *The pitcher photographed has a collar of Moorish design, and although the design on the body seems oriental, the overall effect, especially on the plates is Art Nouveau. It is difficult to date the pattern because Cauldon Ltd. used an old Ridgway mark. English, Mk. 822, L.V. c. 1910.*

An example has been found marked JR & Co. (John Ridgeway & Co., Mk. 3259a, E.V., 1841-1855)

page 165 **"DUCHESS"** *This pattern is not Art Nouveau, it is floral, see correct listing in the book.*

page 165 **"OSBORNE"** *by Rathbone. This is a correct description of the pattern and photograph of a plate in the author's collection.*

This gilt edged scalloped plate carries its design on the rim only. The upper edge encircled with a string of little flowers and beads. The main design consists of five groups of a trio of full blown roses and these are separated by Art Nouveau triangular design of scrolls and flowers. The well is encircled by a necklace of garlanded beads and stylized fleur-de-lis.

English, Marked TR & Co., Mk. 3205, L.V., c. 1910

BUCCARA, UNGLAZED RED STONEWARE TEAPOT, MING.

A FOLIO OF DRAWINGS

By

BETSY McGLONE HENDERSHOT

ARTIST

LOUISVILLE, KENTUCKY

DRAWINGS FROM PHOTOGRAPHS OF THE COLLECTION OF
EDITH T. MILLER
PENNSYLVANIA

PLATE XIII

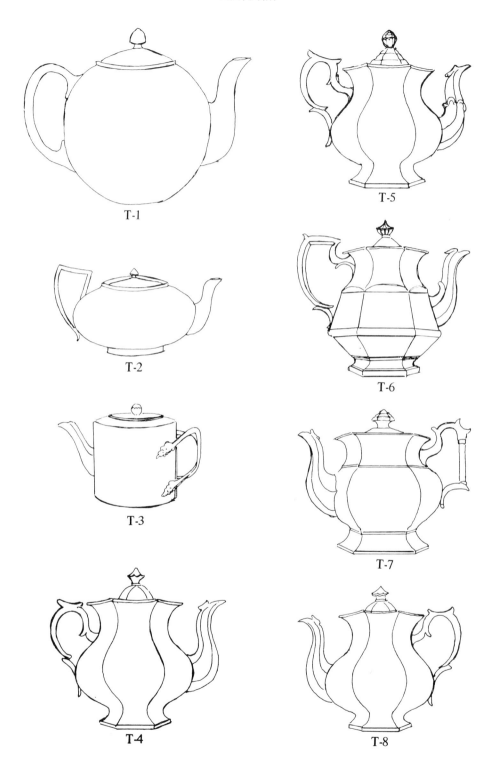

T-1

T-2

T-3

T-4

T-5

T-6

T-7

T-8

PLATE XIV

T-9

T-13

T-10

T-14

T-11

T-15

T-12

T-16

PLATE XV

S-1

S-4

S-2

S-5

S-3

S-6

S-7

PLATE XVI

S-8

S-11

S-9

S-12

S-10

S-13

S-14

PLATE XIX

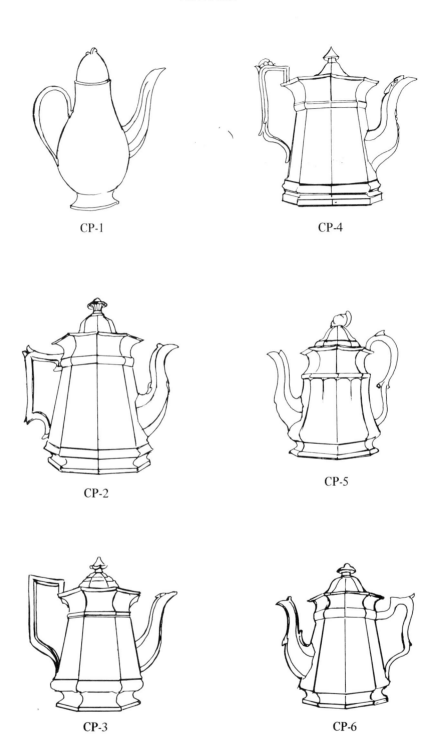

CP-1

CP-4

CP-2

CP-5

CP-3

CP-6

PLATE XX

CP-7

CP-10

CP-8

CP-11

CP-9

CP-12

PLATE XVII

C-1

C-4

C-2

C-5

C-3

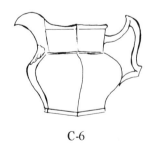

C-6

PLATE XVIII

C-7

C-9

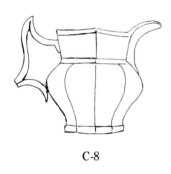

C-8

C-10

C-11

PLATE XXI

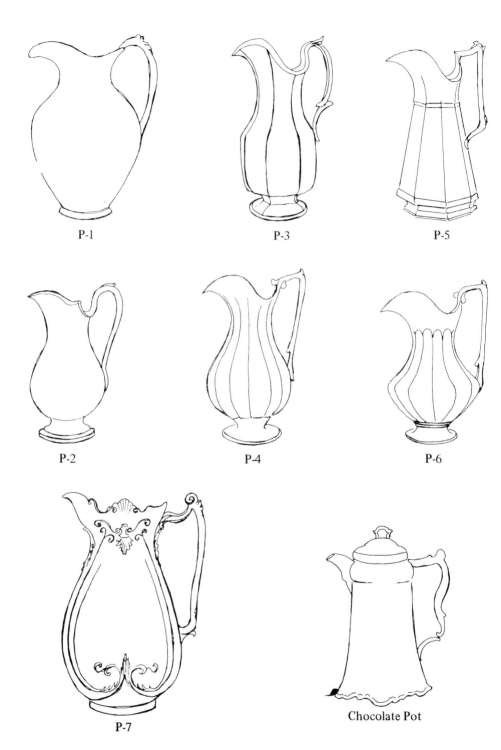

P-1

P-3

P-5

P-2

P-4

P-6

P-7

Chocolate Pot

*Brush-Stroke
Painted Category*

There are many simple decorative patterns found on Flow Blue ware that were not achieved by the use of the transfer printing process. Numerous designs dating from the early part of the nineteenth century can be found that were hand brushed with cobalt on the biscuit before transfers were invented, and after that when some potters found hand labor more economical than the cost of transfers. "Heath's Flower", on page 182 of Book I is an example of this technique, and the pattern dates c. 1830. The process, however, consisting of either freehand drawing, or perhaps the use of stencils, was used throughout the Victorian age and can date as late as 1900, as is the case of the various Spinach patterns.

The designs resembling strawberries have gained their names among collectors because of the obvious details of the painted fruit. Other patterns are more elusive to describe because they bear little relationship to realism. It is difficult to buy and sell this type of Flow Blue because the usual description is "primitive' or "stoneware with a coarse blue design".

Therefore, in compiling this category, we will attempt to give names to the examples depicted of the conventionalized flower, fruit, leaf, and plant patterns which have been brought to our attention to date. Whenever possible, we will date the piece and state the name of the maker. These descriptive titles are not intended to be arbitrary, but are offered in order to make correspondence possible between collectors in this specialized field.

ASTER AND GRAPESHOT
Made by Joseph Clementson
English, marked Clementson, Shelton
like Mk. 910b, E.V., c. 1840

**BELL BORDER WITH
FLOWER AND FERN**

BLEEDING HEART

BLUEBELL WITH CHERRY BORDER

Marked "Stone China" (impressed). Could be James Edwards, English, E.V. c. 1845

BLUEBELL AND GRAPES
WITH CHERRY BORDER

CHERRY

CROSSED BANDS

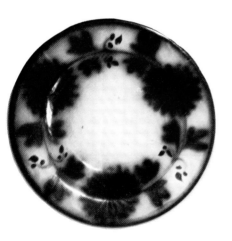

DAHLIA

There is copper lustre placed over the flowers and leaves on this plate. Also, red and green leaves have been added to the stems.

DAISY

This pattern is marked "Sociate Cer-amique" and Maastricht. It is Dutch L.V. c. 1891

DAISY SEVEN PETALS

DIAMOND LEAF CROSS

DOT FLOWER

FERN

FERN AND BAR

This plate is marked "Stone China" (impressed). Could be James Edwards, English, E.V. c. 1845

FERN AND TULIP

GRAPES

GRAPES AND LEAVES WITH BLUE BAND

LEAF AND SWAG

LEAVES AND BAR

LOTUS AND LEAVES

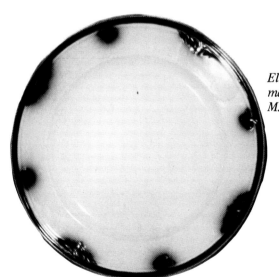

LUSTRE BAND
Marked "E.F.&Co." This is the mark of
Elsmore and Forster. The plate is also
marked "Improved Opaque China". English,
M.V. c. 1860

MALTESE CROSS BAND AND STRIPE

PEACH BLOSSOM

Marked "Pearl" (impressed) and dated July 1851. Made by Charles Collinson & Co. English, marked C. Collinson & Co., Mk. 1013, M.V., c. 1860

POSY WREATH

RED BIRD

The design of this cup is painted in blue except for the little bird which is painted in red.

REEDS AND FLOWERS

REGOUT'S FLOWER

This pattern was misplaced in Book I in Art Nouveau. It is definitely hand painted. The outside is decorated with a fan of leaves and three small flowers on stems, with stylized leaves between them. The inside of the bowl has a picture of the three flowers in the center. The top inside border is composed of a turkey feather design. The bowl is Dutch, marked P.R.(Petrus Regout), L.V. c. 1900

SEA WEED

SPINACH III

Marked "LA FAIENCERIE DE NIMY". No such mark located. It was probably the mark of a pottery since disappeared in Belgium.

SPINACH WITH CIRCLED FLOWER

Dutch, marked Societe Ceramique, Maastricht. L.V., c. 1891

STICK SPATTER

This pitcher is decorated with a zig zag pattern. Directly under this is a row of small crosses. These designs and the stars on the body were achieved by cutting a piece of sponge into the desired shape, attaching this to a stick, which was dropped into dry pigment, then stamped on the china.

THREE PETALS AND LEAVES

TULIP AND SPRIG

Marked "T. Walker" (impressed). Made by Thomas Walker, in England, E.V. c. 1845

TULIPS AND LEAVES

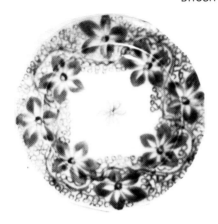

VINCA AND BEADS

WHEEL

This is a so called "gaudy" pattern. The dish is very flown with cobalt; the blue bars are hand painted and outlined with gold; the leafy vertical bars are painted in dark red.

WILD STRAWBERRY

PLATE XXII

Supper Set "Water Nymph" by Wedgwood. Photograph Courtesy of Frank Vander Berge, Amsterdam, Holland.

PLATE XXIII

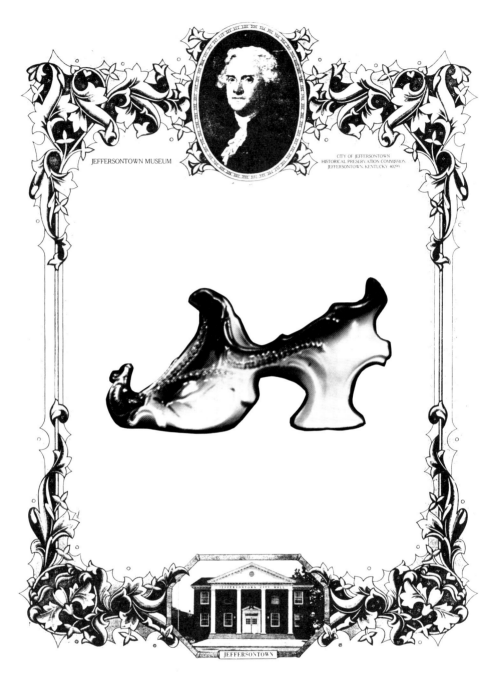

JEFFERSONTOWN MUSEUM

CITY OF JEFFERSONTOWN
HISTORICAL PRESERVATION COMMISSION
JEFFERSONTOWN, KENTUCKY 40299

JEFFERSONTOWN

Slipper with ornate gold trim. Length, 6½ inches. Maker unknown. Provenance indicates Austrian origin.

Miscellaneous Category

ACME

Probably made by Sampson Hancock & Sons

The entire body of this scalloped gilt-edged dish is fluted with rounded vertical lines from edge to center. The surface is covered with a pattern of small wild roses with leaves and a light tracery of stems. Gold lustre has been sprayed over most of the background.

A wide blue band has been painted across the diameter of the plate, and the center part of the band, as it crosses the well, has been extended into a circle. Scallops alongside the band are gold.

English, marked S.H. & Co. Mk. 1929, L.V., c. 1900.

ACORN

Made by Furnivals

This unusual pitcher and basin set is printed with overscaled oak leaves and acorns. The edge of the double lipped pitcher is scalloped and embossed with shells and fluting. The basket type handle is embossed with ridges. The scalloped bowl is oval shaped and the pattern has been placed both on the outside and inside of its surfaces. Gold has been painted around the rim of both pticher and basin.

English, marked as above, MK. 1652, L.V., c. 1900

ADAMS
Made by Wood & Sons

This pitcher is decorated in the restrained neoclassic style that Robert Adams made famous in the 1770s. The upper bands are composed of small formalized bell flowers, as are the large garlands and double sprays that surround the oval floral medallions that are clearly from this school. Small beaded swags circle the top of the body of the vessel and unite the principal designs.

English, marked as above, Predates 1910, L.V., c. 1907

ALBION
Made by W. & E. Corn

This unevenly scalloped plate is embossed with wave forms and scrolls. The design is printed on the rim in a very dark blue. The outer edge consists of straight vertical lines. Large foliated scrolls printed in a lighter blue forms crosses, swirls and floral forms on the rim which give a tapestry effect. The well is detailed with a wreath of tiny flowers and scrolls.

Albion is an archaic word meaning Britain.

English, marked as above, Mk. 1113, L.V., c. 1900

ALEXANDRA

Made by S. Hancock & Sons

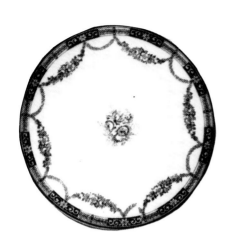

The design on this plate is printed in black and in a slate blue that has a purple cast.

The outer edge is banded with oblong medallions containing a flower and scrolls and these alternate with bands of laurel leaves intersected by a diamond.

The pattern on the rim consists of swags of laurel leaves and garlands of flowers.

The central bouquet is composed of a mixture of roses, dahlias, forget-me-nots and sprigs.

English, marked as above, like Mk. 1935, L.V., c. 1910

ANTIQUE BOTTLE

Made by John Meir & Son

The milk or water pitcher photographed is decorated at the top, both inside and on the outer surface by a sprawling pattern of scrolls, flowers and leaves.

The pattern gains its name because of the round bottle-shaped vased that is depicted at the left. It is filled with branches of an overscaled lotus-type flower and leaves. At the right there is a fence leading to a bank planted with trees, shrubs and flowers.

The foot rim is visible and is decorated with small scrolls.

The backstamp pictures several bottles around a scroll that bears the name above.

English, marked J.M.&S Mk. 2633, probably E.V. or M.V.

234

ARABESQUE
Made by G. Kent

The plant stand pictured has a collar of scrolls and a base with the same design. A larger version of the design appears above the waist of the body.

The main design is composed of a central ovoid medallion that resembles a wheel and spokes. Four large pairs of ram horn scrolls extend from the central oval, and these are joined by four stylized lotus flowers.

The design is printed in cobalt, and rouge-de-fer has been applied over the glaze to accent the central design and the borders.

English, marked in script "G. Kent, Sole Manufacturer, 199 High Halborn, F. Hahn Danchell's Patent", No such mark located.

ARABIC
Made by James Edwards

This small dish is eight sided and the top quarter inch of its edge is flat before the rim descends to the well. Small scrolls are placed in a symmetrical pattern around the rim. The well is defined by a comb tooth design. The central design is a fancy greek cross with spear shaped points and a rosette in its center. It is surrounded by a pattern of tiny scrolls.

English, marked JE, dated 1842, Mk. 1449, E.V., c. 1842

ASTORIA
Made by Upper Hanley Pottery

This pattern covers the entire surface of the slightly scalloped, gilt edged and embossed plate photographed. The pattern consists of small flowers, round bud forms and dark shaggy leaves. It is very much like "Hawthorne" made by the Mercer Pottery in the United States.

English, marked as above, Mk. 3928, L.V., c. 1895

235

AURORA
Made by Francis Morley & Co.

This heavy old plate is indented on its dark edge at four places. Three sprawling designs of scrolls and leaves and flowers alternate on the rim with three trefoil designs composed of scrolls.

The well is almost filled with a pattern of very dark scrolls and leaves and lighter stylized flowers and buds done in the oriental fashion.

English, marked, F.M. & Co., Mk. 2760, E.V., c. 1845

BAMBOO
Made by Samuel Alcock & Co.

Pale grass green has been placed on the rim of this irregulary scalloped plate. The blue leaf design around the outer edge has been hand painted over the green.

The center design is transfer printed in cobalt and there are sprigs on the reverse side of the plate which are also transfer printed.

The central scene shows tall bamboo trees and two large butterflies and a small insect flying above the tree tops.

There is some pale green present in the center of the design. Gold paint has been placed over the leaves on the rim and also on part of the well picture.

English, marked S.A. & Co., Mk. 75, E.V., c. 1845.

BOUQUET
Made by William Brownfield

The cake plate photographed is slightly scalloped and the edge is embossed and printed with foliated scrolls. The handles are made of somewhat larger scrolls.

The well is encircled by a twisted ribbon that wreaths around several different cultivated flowers. The central medallion is composed of a six petalled stylized flower.

English, marked W.B., Mk. 660, dated 1851, E.V., c. 1851

BRAZIL

Made by W. H. Grindley

This unevenly scalloped plate is detailed with tiny dot embossing. A pattern of very dark shaggy leaves forms a wreath around the upper rim and small paler blue flowers appear on the lower rim and enter the well.

In the center is a pinwheel made of the leaves, surrounded by a wreath of sprigs.

English, marked as above, Mk. 1842, L.V., c. 1891

BRYONIA

Made by Paul Utzshneider & Co.

This saucer has a fluted upper rim and the outer edge is gilded.

The pattern is of grape leaves printed in two shades of blue, one a slate blue and the other a very dark cobalt. Gold has been placed over the darker leaves.

German, marked U & C, See Thorn (pg. 13, Mk. 14), L.V., pre 1891.

BURLINGTON

Possibly made by Cauldon

This cake plate is evenly scalloped and its embossed handles are detailed with heavy gold paint.

The rim design consists of circular running scrolls. The well is encircled by a plain dark line and then an inner row of semi-ovals and straight lines and dots that form a rounded picket effect.

In the center a wheel is formed by the same circular scrolls.

English, registered date of December 4, 1845, like mark in Kovel page 248 (m). This mark was used by Cauldon and since this backstamp is not marked England the piece dates before 1891, and may date to the time of Brown-Westhead Moore & Co. (1859). The time of registry of the pattern may not be the date of the plate, M.V., c. 1860.

237

BUTE
Made by Ford & Sons

The pattern on this platter is a combination of Baroque corner reserves that contain treillage and an Art Nouveau rendition of stylized flowers and scrolls that is placed on the four sides of the dish. These diverse elements are linked by a pair of scrolls under the corner design and garlands of beads under the floral patterns.

Bute is the name of a county in Scotland.

English, marked F. & Son, Mk. 1585, L.V., c. 1900.

CANNISTER
Maker Unknown

The tea cannister shown here is decorated with a soft flowing blue in the stylized pattern of lotus blossoms, leaves and sprigs that is associated with the "Meissen" patterns.

German, marked Germany, L.V., c. 1891.

CANTON VINE
Maker Unknown

The shell shaped relish dish pictured is very flown over its entire body. The overprinting consists of trailing vines that terminate in small stylized flowers.

English, E.V., c. 1845

CHAPLET
Made by J. & C. Meakin

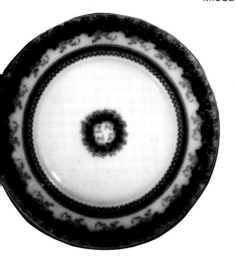

The pigment used on this plate is greyish blue. The edge is embossed with tiny dots and crosses from which small dotted swags surround the upper rim, which is printed with a wreath of foliated scrolls and shaggy flowers from which sprigs extend over the middle part of the rim. The bottom of the rim is encircled three times. First with printed beading, secondly with a narrow gold band, and third a design of scallops, dots and a pointed edge that forms a lacy wreath. This is not printed on the well, it is actually printed on the rim.

A baroque medallion of scrolls, flowers and sprigs is placed in the center.

English, marked as above, Mk. 2599, Registry #33283, L.V., c. 1900

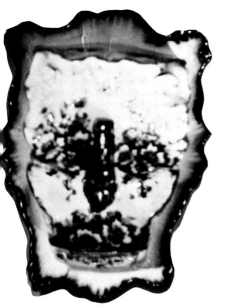

CHEESE DISH II
Maker Unknown

The wedge shaped cheese dish photographed is scalloped, fluted and gilded. The cover is decorated with a pattern of corn flowers.

English, L.V., c. 1880-1890

CHINESE PLANT
Made by A. S. Knight

The saucer photographed combines a realistic drawing of a clematis type flower and an oriental rendition of tendrils and plant base. The border design contains large foliated scrolls and a gothic type pattern of oak leaves and small pointed arch forms.

English, marked as above with an impressed rosette, no mark located, E.V., c. 1845.

CLUNY
Made by Furnivals, Ltd.

There is no backstamp on this small platter nor on another dish bearing the same design. This name will be used to catalogue the pattern which appears only on the rim. The edge is scalloped, beaded and gilded. Scrolled floral embossing is placed around the upper part of the rim.

Dark acanthus leaves are situated at the top of the rim. These are separated by a diamond lacy pattern that is edged with arches and pendant tabs, and is fringed. Beneath the arches there are small bouquets that are flanked by sprigs that achieve a garland effect.

English, marked as above, like Mk. 1658a, L.V., c. 1910

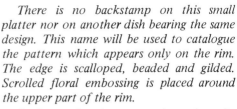

COCKATOO
Made by Villeroy & Boch

Two birds are perched on a limb of a peach tree in this pattern picture. They are surrounded by naturalistic, but overscaled flowers and leaves. Each bird has the typical crest of the cockatoo.

The border, (not shown) is set inside the top rim of the cup. The design consists of three shield shaped foliated cartouches that are separated by a row of small daisies that are placed over a row of smaller acanthus shapes and large oval lace-like loops.

The correct title is INDIA. (See BIRDS AT FOUNTAIN, this book page 84.)

German, marked V&B, L.V., c. 1880

CORAL

Made by Johnson Bros.

This small bowl is unevenly scalloped and has a wide band of floral and bead embossing. The design is a fairly stylized vine-like pattern of foliated scrolls and very small stylized five petalled flowers. This design enters partially into the well. The pattern has nothing to do with a design of real coral formations. This pattern may be borderline.

English, marked as above, like Mk. 2177, L. V., c. 1900.

CORBEILLE

Possibly made by C. Meigh

The word 'corbeille' means a sculptured ornament in the form of a basket.

This plate has pictures of flower filled baskets around the rim, and these alternate with a geometrical pyramid filled with a diamond wicker pattern. The edge is outlined by a band of the same pattern.

A large basket of woven wicker appears in the well. It has a tall curved handle composed of scrolls, and it is filled with peonies and leaves. The basket rests on top of a platform of wavy scrolls and flowers. An exotic bird is perched at left and a butterfly is placed above him.

English, marked impressed "Improved Stone", E. V., c. 1849.

CORINTHIAN

Maker Unknown

The rim and part of the well of this plate are covered with a thick design of leafy snail-like scrolls. Beneath these there is a row of stylized acanthus leaves. These are printed in a very dark cobalt over a greenish ground.

The center of the dish is marked by a double circle of simple blue bands on a white field.

There is no name on this plate, this name is used to catalogue the pattern.

CRAWFORD RANGES

Made by Sampson Bridgwood & Son

Store keepers and manufactures representatives gave away advertising items such as this dish, toward the end of the nineteenth century.

The border on the plate is ornate, with four large cartouches containing corncopias full of fruit and large foliated scrolls. These are separated by small oval reserves containing an elaborate letter C on a field of shell patterns.

The well is encircled by a wreath of scallop shells and thick scrolls.

The words in the middle carry the message "Crawford Cooking Ranges".

The backstamp reads "Made for the Walker and Pratt Manufacturing Company, Boston, Massachusetts".

English, marked S.B.&S., Mk. 595, L.V., c. 1885

CUBA

Possibly Made by Davenport

This plate is twelve sided and panelled. The border design extends halfway into the well. The rim pattern consists of small flowers set within reserves formed by foliated scrolls, these are separated by dark fan-like patterns sprayed out over arch forms.

The center pattern is oriental in feeling and consists of an overscaled stylized flower in the left foreground and a flight of stairs leading to a gazebo and a tower structure at right.

Probably English, marked with a printed anchor, probably E.V., c. 1845

242

DALIAH

Made by Edward Challinor

The rim of this plate is printed with panelled zig zag lines that form a sort of geometric scallop. At four equal distance spots there are scrolls and a leaf form and two small stylized flowers and leaves. These enter the well.

The center of the well is occupied by a large, dark, stylized dahlia and stems with realistic paler leaves.

English, marked E.C., Mk. 835, E.V., c. 1850.

DELMAR

Made by W. H. Grindley

The unevenly scalloped edge of this plate is set off by scroll and shell embossing.

The design is placed primarily on the rim and consists of groups of blackberries and leaves on thorny stems.

English, marked as above, Mk. 1842, L.V., c. 1891.

DERBY

Made by Furnivals

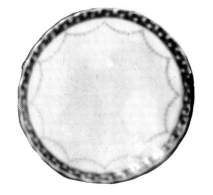

This scalloped plate has an outer edge design of small flowers set on a blue band. Swags of beading are placed from the band to circle the lower rim.

English, marked as above, like Mk. 1658a, Registry #388682, L.V., c. 1902

243

DIANA

Made by J. & G. Meakin

This plate is very slightly scalloped. The outer rim is printed with a border of small flowerets and sprigs. The border is divided in six places with a scrolled vertical bar and between these are pairs of small flowers. The same flowerets are used to form a loose circle around the bottom of the well, and a small spray is centered therein.

English, marked as above, Mk. 2600, L.V., c. 1907

DORIS

Made by Sampson Hancock & Sons

The tray photographed is part of a dresser set which contains a pin tray, a candle holder, a receiver for hair combings and two small octagonal pomade boxes with covers.

The edge design is stylized and composed of four petalled flowers, crosses and bars. A dainty picket design appears under the edge.

The central design is a mirror like figure centered with a bouquet in a vase, imposed on a gold background. This is surmounted by flowers and leaves. The handle is decorated with scrolls and pendants.

A pair of flower baskets, set in scrolls is placed at right and left. A swag of leaves and flowers descends from the scrolls and terminates in pendants.

English, marked ¬s above, Mk. 1935, L.V., c. 1910. ·

DOROTHY

Made by Johnson Bros.

This gilt edged saucer is scalloped and is embellished with two rows of embossing, one of beads and one of a plain line. The outer edge is printed with tiny clovers. The upper rim is decorated with a lace like pattern of scallops and stylized small flowers, while the lower part contains realistic groups of small roses.

The well is outlined by a spear point design.

English, marked as above, Mk. 2177, L.V., c. 1900

DOROTHY

Made by the Upper Hanley Pottery

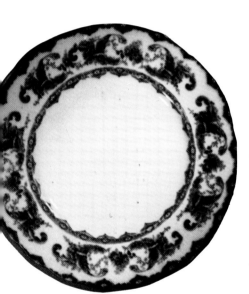

The scalloped plate photographed has comb tooth embossing around the edge and this is further detailed by a dark band of curved triangular forms. The rim is decorated with large feathery scrolls that are bound in pairs by a crown and which are surrounded by small flowers and sprays.

The well is encircled by a row of flowers and the same curved triangular forms that appear on the outer edge.

English, marked as above, Mk. 3928, Registry #354458, L.V., c. 1900

DRESDEN

Made by Villeroy & Bach

The syrup pitcher photographed has a pewter lid and is printed with a Miessen style design of stylized poppies, leaves and buds.

German, Mk. 40, pg. 37, Thorn, L.V., c. 1900

ENGLAND

Made by W. H. Grindley

Pictured on this pitcher are inset scenes of points of interest in England. They are placed on slanting vertical scroll bands over a background of stylized drawings of flowers and leaves. This type of design was popular at the turn of the century; it usually was manufactured in brown and white.

English, marked as above, Mk. 1842, L.V., c. 1891

ERIE

Made by Bourne & Leigh Ltd.

The plate photographed is gently and unevenly scalloped and has very slight embossing.

The design appears on the rim only and on the printed scalloped outer edge and consists of a circular design of small wreaths, each enclosing a flower separated by sprigs. A narrow band of circles is placed mid rim and flowers are twined about this. The lower border is sprinkled with little flowered sprigs.

English, See Ormsbee page 32, Mk. 2, L.V., c. 1900

ETRUSCAN

Made by Wood & Brownfield

The deep dish photographed is unevenly scalloped and the edge is defined by a heavy embossed band. Blue lines are placed over this and foliated scrolls appear at the scallop points.

The pattern is dominated by a large cup-like vase on a pedestal. It has heart shaped handles. There are designs of greek-clad nymphs on the body of the vase which rests upon a platform of stone shapes and is filled with overscaled dahlias, peonies and other exotic flowers. These spill over the rim and across the center of the plate. At the right an oriental bird flies toward the vase. Sprays of fuchsia and prunus are placed on the rim in order to complete the circular design.

English, marked W & B, Mk. 4242, E.V., c. 1845

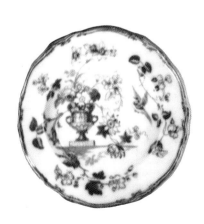

FESTOON

Made by W. H. Grindley

The design on this pitcher is printed in a slate blue. The border around the upper part is composed of trailing maple leaves and a scalloped ribbon. This band is also embossed with beading and small floral scrolls.

The pattern on the body, from which the name is derived, is composed of draped festoons of bell flowers which surround a single silhouetted bell flower with leaves. This same design appears around the collar.

English, Marked as above, Mk. 1842, L.V., c. 1891.

FESTOON

Made by Arthur J. Wilkinson

This covered vegetable dish has garlands of flowers connected with flowing ribbons. The edge of the bowl and lid are gently scalloped and the lid is embossed and beaded around a left-flowing scroll that surrounds the handle, which is also defined by a wreath of small flowers and a brocaded band.

English, marked Royal Staffordshire Pottery, Mk. 4170, L.V., c. 1907

FLEUR-DE-LIS

Made by W. T. Copeland & Sons

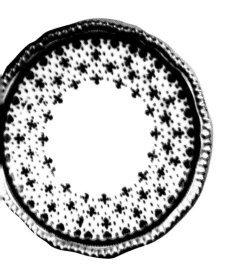

The scalloped edge of this plate is deeply ridged to give a gadroon effect and this ridge is covered with gold. The upper part of the rim is decorated with a rope design and a scalloped linear border contained by a trefoil leaf design and beads. The main design consists of three concentric rows of fleur-de-lis on a dotted field. The design invades the well for over an inch.

English, marked as above, Like Mk. 1075, impressed date, L.V., c. 1894

FLORA

Made by Thomas Walker

A large sunflower, an equally large lily, buds and leaves are placed in the center of this cup plate. The twelve sided and paneled rim is covered with sponge work. The sponged ware effect is obtained by dabbing the colours on to the surface with a sponge.

This pattern is found most often in mulberry and a pale blue.

English, marked (impressed) Thos. Walker, Mk. 3928A, E.V., c. 1845

FLORENTINE

Mady by Thomas Furnival & Sons

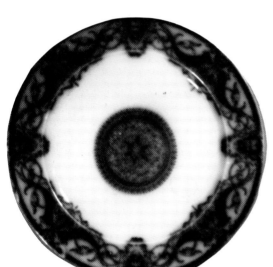

The rim of this plate is edged in a beaded dark blue band. At four places on the rim there are mask designs of a bearded and horned man in a devil's cap. These are draped with garlands. Alternating with the masks is a scroll pattern that is composed of two dolphin forms that meet at a pendant design.

The medallion in the center consists of a six pointed star that is set in a large circle that radiates from a small circle; this is placed in a tracing of flowers and scrolls. A beaded band encloses the design and this in turn is circumscribed by a spear point design of diamond points and small straight lines.

English, marked T. Furnival & Sons, Register dated 1868, (Furnival and Sons started in business in 1871) M.V., c. 1871

FLORIS

Made by Ford & Son

This rectangular platter is printed on its edge with a band of fleur-de-lis, scallops and dots. The rim pattern consists of four Reserves containing bouquets (one on each side) consisting of dahlias, buds and foliage. The bottoms of these enter the well. The bouquets are separated by cartouche forms in each corner that are made of scrolls containing a net field on which there is a stylized flower.

English, Marked F. & Sons, Mk. 1585, L.V., c. 1891

FLOWER BASKET
Maker Unknown

This is a picture plate, probably intended for display on the wall or in a cupboard. It is deeply scalloped and fluted with beaded embossing, and gold lustre has been applied around the edge. The central picture covers the entire dish and consists of a large woven basket that has a round bamboo handle. The basket contains a bouquet of peonies, daisies and prunus blossoms.

There is no backstamp on this plate. This name is used to catalogue the pattern.

Probably English, probably M.V., c. 1875-1880

FRANCE
Made by Brown-Westhead, Moore & Co.

This plate is printed in a soft slate blue. The rim is decorated in three reserves that show scenes of Brittany in southern France. These are connected by a decorative band of geometric lines within a border and placed over flowering boughs. The well is detailed with another geometric band. Three birds fly in the center of the well.

English, marked as above, Registry dated 1868, Mk. 679, M. V., c. 1868.

FRUIT BASKET
Made by Thomas Dimmock

Fruit baskets such as this one were used for serving fruit as part of a dessert service. The dish is scalloped at its corners and the slanting inside rim is decorated and edged with a spear point design of fleur-de-lis. Sprays of oriental type flowers are placed around the four upper parts of the dish above the pierced sides.

The pattern is Bamboo, described in Book I on page 13. This bowl is presented so that readers can become aware of the variety of dishes used in Victorian dinners, and specifically the pottery baskets available.

English, marked "D" and Kaolin Ware", Mk. 1298, E.V., c. 1845

GEM
Made by Ralph Hammersley

This saucer is decorated with a stick spatter design of diamonds, dots, and spear points.

The center design pictures an eagle with outstretched wings, head to left, body pointing right. He is perched on an American shield, and a ribbon with E. Pluribus Unum is placed at the bottom of the design.

This pattern is also known as Eagle & Shield. It should be mentioned that an eagle is incorporated in the backstamp also.

English, marked as above, also marked "U.S. Consulate Service 1868", See Godden, page 305, M.V., c. 1868.

GOTHIC
Made by Charles Meigh & Son

The edge of this deep dish is trimmed with a narrow band of acanthus leaves and dots.

A design of stylized roses is placed on the rim and these alternate with five pair of foliated scrolls. Another large rose is placed in the center of the well. But the dominate feature of this pattern is the circle of gothic arches surrounding the well.

English, marked C.M.&S. and "Improved Stone China", like Mk. 2620, E.V., c. 1855

250

GRAPE VINE PUNCH BOWL
Made by American China Co.

The outside of this bowl is printed with silver blue grapes, leaves and tendrils on a white ground. The same pattern is placed inside the bowl which has a flow blue ground fading from the edge from very dark to pale blue in the center. Gold outlines the scalloped edge.

Acanthus leaves are placed on the pedestal base and this is edged with a solid gold band.

American, marked as above, See Thorn Page 115, Mk. 6, L.V., c. 1896

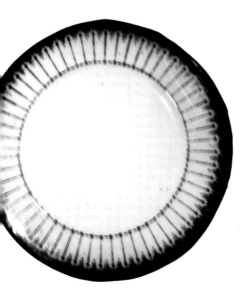

GRECIAN
Made by Ford & Sons Ltd.

This rim pattern consists of a blackish outer band contained by a row of small double scrolls. The well is surrounded by a circle of threaded small quatrefoils. The two designs are connected by vertical lines of tiny beads. Small pointed stylized acanthus leaves are placed at the upper edge between the beaded lines.

English, marked F. & Sons, Mk. 1586, L.V., c. 1908

GRIFFIN

Made by Davenport

The wide rim and sloping sides of this scalloped deep dish are covered with a pattern of swirling foliated scrolls. At four places on the rim the scrolls terminate into the heads of the renditions of the mythical beast, the griffin, who was pictured with the head and wings of an eagle and the body of a lion.

Gold is used to outline the dish's edge and to highlight the griffins and part of the scroll.

The central medallion is composed of three griffin heads with long forked tongues made of scrolls that are pinwheeled around a central rosette.

English, impressed anchor mark, impressed Davenport, dated 1847, Mk. 1179a and 1181a, M.V., c. 1847

HANGING BASKET

Made by William Ridgway & Co.

There is no pattern name on this plate, this name will be used to catalogue the pattern.

The plate is unevenly scalloped. The rim is printed with foliated Baroque scroll reserves filled with a honey-comb diaper pattern. Flowers and sprigs are placed between the scroll pattern and underneath them in such a way that they appear in the well.

A basket is suspended by tasselled cords from one of the scroll designs. It has an ornate scrolled handle that looks like gothic ironwork, and its body is round and short and terminates in a carved pendant. It is filled with large flowers, leaves and tendrils.

A butterfly is placed at the lower right.

English, marked impressed W.R. & Co. and "Opaque Granite", also printed crown mark 3258A, Mk. 3303, E.V., c. 1845

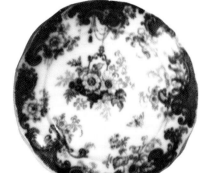

HARROW

Made by Thomas Rathbone & Co.

Harrow is a city in England eleven miles northwest of London. It is the site of the famous boys school founded in 1571 which bears the same name.

The fruit bowl photographed is ornate, it is deeply scalloped, fluted and embossed. A bouquet of Japanese Pinks, placed over some treillage, is pictured in the center of the dish, and four sprays of wild roses are placed around the central motif.

The rim is very dark blue and the colour fades toward the center. Gold lustre has been placed over the floral pattern and around the edge.

English, marked T.R. & Co., Mk. 3204, L.V., c. 1900

HAWTHORNE

Made by Mercer Pottery Company

This bone dish has no name on the backstamp so until it can be found it will be catalogued as Hawthorne.

This is another of Mercer's all over patterns like Paisley (See Book I, page 194).

It has proven to be impossible to find the names of these patterns after inquiry of the location of the old Mercer pattern books at Trenton, New Jersey where the plant was located.

American, See Hartman, page 116, Mk. 19, L.V., c. 1890

HERON

Made by Charles Meigh

The scalloped edge of this plate is outlined by a narrow border of criss cross
lozenges and four small oval medallions. The
rim is printed with four stylized lotus
flowers, leaves and buds.

In the center the great heron stands a
little to the left. His crested head is turned
to the left as he carries small leaves. At right
is an overscaled stylized flower.

English, marked C.M., Mk. 2618, E.V., c.
1840

HERON

Made by G. W. Turner & Sons

The scene on this plate depicts part of a
pond afloat with water lilies and pads. Marsh
grass grows from it and a tall oak tree stump,
twined with ivy is placed along the left rim
and circles toward the top of the dish. At
the right a shorter group of reeds, flowers
and leaves is placed on the rim.

A large heron stands in the right foreground. Behind him in the middle another
heron is fishing with his beak, and a third
member of the family is flying above the
scene.

English, marked G.W.T. & Sons, Mk.
3891, M.V., c. 1873

IMPERIAL

Made by William Adderly & Co.

This soup dish is gently scalloped and
there is scroll embossing on the rim at six
equi-distant places. The design appears on
the rim and consists of royal crowns that
alternate with double fruit-filled cornucopias. These are linked by garlands of roses.
The printing is in slate blue.

English, marked W.A.A. & Co., Mk. 49,
Registry #356790, L.V., c. 1900

JAPANESE SCROLL

Possibly made by Deakin & Son

This platter is unevenly scalloped and the edge which is heavily embossed is covered with cobalt.

The rim pattern consists of a wreath of thick foliated scrolls. The central oval medallion is surrounded by the same type of scrolls.

English, marked impressed "Pearl", E.V., c. 1840

JEWEL

Made by John Maddock & Sons

The scalloped edge of this plate is outlined in gold and a band of printed hair pin loops.

The design on the border consists of eight heart shaped cartouches containing a foliated cross design. These are joined by a baroque design of foliated scrolls and fleur-de-lis over double bell-flower forms.

The rim design is contained at the top and bottom by double white lines and the well is encircled with a wreath of the hair pin design finished toward the center with spear points.

English, marked as above, Mk. 2463, L.V., c. 1895

JEWEL

Made by John Tams

The simple rim design is edged by a narrow key border and consists of pendant shaped medallions containing a rose. A small oblong strip flanks every other pendant and alternates with roses used in the same way. The designs are linked by garlands of beads.

English, marked "Crown Pottery" and J.T., Mk. 3793, Registry #624328, M.V., c. 1875

255

JEWELL
Made by Ford & Sons

The bowl is oval shaped and is deeply scalloped. Larger scallops form the handles. The body of the vessel is embossed with shells and gold has been placed over this. The design consists of large poppies which are placed on both the inside and outside surfaces.

English, marked F. & Sons, Mk. 1582, L.V., c. 1892.

KENT
Made by W. H. Grindley

This scalloped gilt edged plate combines elements of floral and baroque designs. It is embossed at six points on the rim with large fleur-de-lis and curving scrolls. These are printed over with cobalt. Small lighter blue floral swags and sprays are placed on the lower part of the rim. The well is encircled by a wreath of tiny pointed scallops.

The main design is star shaped and consists of six curving dark lines that terminate in points. These surround a wreath of small stylized flowers from which six large flowers extend into the dark curves.

English, marked as above, Mk. 1842, L.V., c. 1891

MABEL
Made by Charles Allerton & Sons

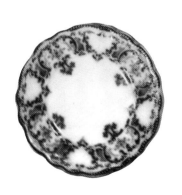

This plate is unevenly scalloped and its dark edge is trimmed with beaded embossing. Floral and scroll embossing has also been placed on the upper rim.

The pattern consists of four oval medallions that contain a single rose. At the base of each is a triangular spade-like pattern that protrudes into the well. Each medallion is separated from the other by a cartouche space that is formed by angular dark reserves and darker scrolls. These too are based on a triangular design that extends toward the well.

English, marked as above, Mk. 88, L.V., c. 1905

MADRAS

Made by Upper Hanley Pottery Company

This pattern is almost identical to "Delph" made by Wood & Sons, except that there are three large sprays of flowers around this rim as compared to shorter sprigs and flowers on the Delph pattern.

The edge is outlined by a border of diamond lozenge design. Stylized flowers in the oriental manner are placed on the rim. The well is outlined by a band like that around the edge. A basket with a tall handle is placed in the center. This is filled with stylized flowers.

English, marked as above, mark 3928, L.V., c. 1900

MALTA

Made by W. H. Grindley & Company

The greyish blue printing on this dish is used in a Japanese inspired design. The outer geometric pattern on the border is composed of triangles and dots. The rim pattern shows a tracing of small flowers over a dotted background divided by triangular lines. A scalloped edge encircles the upper well.

The center medallion is a repetition of the edge design encircled by the elements of the floral border.

English, marked as above, like Mk. 1842, Registry #69160, L.V., c. 1880

MEISSEN

Made by Minton

The deep dish photographed is very gently and irregularly scalloped. The outer edge is detailed with a printed scrolled border that is shaded with vertical lines. Small sprigs and flowers are placed touching this around the upper rim.

The center design which covers the deep well is printed upon the sloping sides and consists of a large formalized and oriental bouquet of chrysanthemums and bamboo stalks with shaggy leaves and buds which is placed behind a vase of coral-like stone designs. Some berry clusters are depicted at lower right.

English, marked M. & Co., impressed "New Stone", marked BB (Best Body), E.V. c. 1850

MINWOOD

Made by Henry Alcock & Company

The design on this dish appears only on the rim and is printed in slate blue. Narrow gold lines outline the outer circle of a stylized wreath of small leaves. A band of snail shaped scrolls covers the lower part of the rim.

English, marked as above, Mk. 65, L.V., c. 1891

NORTHUMBERLAND

Made by Fell & Company

The name given this pattern is chosen in order to show the design. Thomas Fell and Company was the pottery who made this pattern, and this company was located in New Castle upon Tyne, Northumberland.

The rim of the platter is decorated with eight rounded cartouches centered with a square cross surrounded by scrolls and terminated at the bottom by a spear point that enters the well. These round forms are separated by triangular scroll designs that also terminate in a point toward the well.

The central oval medallion is centered by a cross surrounded by feathery scrolls.

English, marked impressed "Porcelain Opaque", Impressed "Fell & Co.", like Mk. 1535, probably M.V.

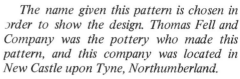

ONION

Made by Allertons

This pattern is identical to "Holland" by Johnson Bros., see page 182, Volume I.

It is another rendition of the oriental pattern copied at Meissen and mistakenly called Onion when the workers mistook the round peach forms for oinions.

English, marked as above, L.V., c. 1891

OSBORNE

Made by John Ridgway, Bates & Company

The design on this plate is composed of various scroll designs. A dark and bold narrow line of foliated scrolls flank a star and petal circle. These alternate with a pale blue cartouche design that encloses a diamond shape of stylized bell flowers. These cartouches are linked to both a circle on the outer edge of the plate and an inner circle on the upper edge of the well. The well is further defined by a narrow dark band and small scrolls.

The central medallion is composed of a dark star-shaped central star made up of stylized bell flowers. This is confined within a light blue and rounded design that has fleur-de-lis incorporated within its five petals and also five small bell flowers and scrolls.

English, marked J.R.B. & Co., Mk. 3269, E.V., c. 1856

PAR

Made by Brown-Westhead, Moore & Co.

The deep dish photographed has a border of printed stylized and lined scallops. The pattern appears on four sides of the rim and consists of stylized leaves, flowers and tendrils. From each of these a pendant extends into the well. The main patterns are separated by curved lines and inverted outlined hearts.

English, marked as above, Pattern registered in December, 1879, Mark 679, M.V., c. 1879

PARISIAN

Made by Samuel Keeling & Co.

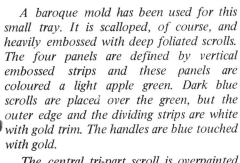

A baroque mold has been used for this small tray. It is scalloped, of course, and heavily embossed with deep foliated scrolls. The four panels are defined by vertical embossed strips and these panels are coloured a light apple green. Dark blue scrolls are placed over the green, but the outer edge and the dividing strips are white with gold trim. The handles are blue touched with gold.

The central tri-part scroll is overpainted with a gold flower at its center.

English, marked S.K. & Co., impressed in octagon "New Stone", Mk. 2247, E.V., c. 1845

PARROT

Maker Unknown

This is a large fern stand that is 36 inches high. It is made on a graduated base with alternating vertical stripes. Pictured on one side is a peacock and a stone ball amidst an overgrown garden. On the side pictured is a fighting parrot poised in a rose bush. The top of the pedestal also carries a picture of the parrot.

There is no backstamp. This name is used to catalogue the pattern.

The stand is dated January, 1860.

Probably English, probably M.V., c. 1860

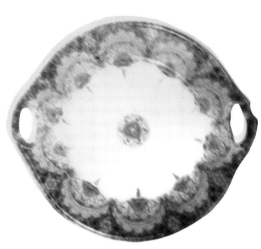

PERSIAN FANS
Made by Utschneider

This cake plate is decorated with a rim design of fan shapes placed against a background of flowers.

The central medallion is composed of double triangles set in a stylized flower form such as seen in Persian art. Gold has been placed over the various pattern elements.

There is no pattern name on the backstamp. This name is used to catalogue the pattern.

German, marked Sarraguemines and a shield mark, See Thorn, page 13, Mk. 19, L.V., c. 1891

PERSIAN MEDALLION
Possibly made by Utschneider

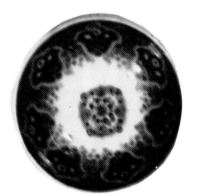

This deep saucer is patterned on the rim with a solid background of small flowers. Inset are shield shaped medallions containing three flowers. These forms are outlined in gilt as are the flowers and stems.

The center medallions is composed of four sides and contains a stylized flower with a pair of dots on each side and a central blossom surrounded by eight lily forms.

There is no pattern name on the backstamp. This name is used to catalogue the pattern.

German, marked "Superior" and W Germany, L.V., c. 1891

PERSIAN SCROLL
Made by Utschneider

The bowl pictured is printed in two toned blue. The pattern is somewhat reminescent of Persian Moss by the same potter. The outer edge is encircled by a very dark band and from this large scrolls that end in a sharp upturn descend toward the well.

The background is composed of mossy swirls and small angular flowers. The border is much like designs seen in prints from India.

The center snowflake pattern is composed of a central eight pointed figure and from this eight spokes radiate. These are made of the same flowers as used in the border and here they are placed on straight stems with small leafy curls that give a leaf effect.

This plate is unmarked except for the shield. We will use this name for cataloguing purposes.

German, marked Sarraguemines with a shield mark, See Thorn page 13, Mk. 19, L.V., c. 1891

PLATA
Made by Petrus Regout

This lily of the valley bulb bowl is printed in slate blue. The outer rim is decorated with a circle of gold that outlines an edging of ovals and dots.

The top of the bowl is decorated with a circle of leafy double wreaths, and the foot is encircled with the same edging of ovals and dots that appear on the top edge.

Dutch, marked as above, marked Maastricht Holland, L.V., c. 1891

POMONA

Made by Brown-Westhead & Moore

This relish dish is scalloped. It is printed in a greyish blue with an all over pattern of cherries and cherry blossoms, leaves and stems.

English, marked as above, Mk. 679, M.V., c. 1862

PRINCESS

Made by James Beech

The unevenly scalloped edge of this plate is outlined with a narrow dark border and a thin gold stripe. The pattern derives its name from three equally spaced small oval medallions that contain a profile portrait of a girl. These are wreathed with roses and are separated by a double pattern of bell flowers, swags and wreathed floral circles and a floral pendant design.

The well is set off by a wreath of leafy scrolls and dots.

English, marked as above, Mk. 314, M.V., c. 1877

QUEBEC

Possibly Made by Utschneider & Company

This design is of stylized flowers set within arches composed of light blue lines against a dark cobalt ground. A continuous wreath of small flowers is set around the bottom of the design on the lower part of the rim.

German, marked ⟨W⟩ and a shield mark, See Hartman, page 74, mark 6, L.V., c. 1891

QUEEN

Made by T. Rathbone & Company

This gently scalloped plate has an edging of bell flowers. The design is placed on the rim and consists of a pair of ferns and scrolls above a circle. This design alternates with the same scrolls and ferns that are used over a pendant design consisting of three small roses. The two design elements are connected with swags of full blown roses. The rose garlands enter the well.

English, marked as above, Mk. 3205, L.V., c. 1910

RACINE

Made by Allerton

This unevenly scalloped dish is embossed with small scrolls and its outer edge is defined with a narrow dark band.

The rim is decorated with six foliated cartouche forms. In three of these the interior space is clear and the space in the other three is filled with heraldic type plumes and embellishment, such as seen in coats of arms.

English, marked as above, Mk. 88, L.V., c. 1905

REGINA

Made by the Société Ceramique

The sauce dish photographed is slightly scalloped and the edge is beaded.

The design is Moorish inspired and consists of flower forms set in curved and pointed arches. Small flowers are placed on the outer part of the rim between the arch patterns.

Dutch, marked as above, L.V., c. 1891

265

RHINE GRAPE

Possibly Made by Utschneider

This large saucer is scalloped and its edge is outlined with deep embossed scrolls and vertical rows of bell flowers.

The slate blue pattern of grapes, tendrils, stems and leaves is placed asymmetrically on three sides of the rim and enters the well.

There is no name on the backstamp. This name is used to catalogue the pattern.

German, marked Germany with a shield, L.V., c. 1891

ROSEBUD

Made by Grove & Stark

This pattern is in typical late Victorian taste. The open scroll at the right shows two children standing on a dock. The scroll is surrounded by mossy rosebuds and a pair of small birds are perched on top of it.

At the left there is a bird in flight, at top a pair of children's balls, and in the foreground there is another scene showing two little children at play.

English, marked G. & S., Mk. 1855, Pattern Registered September, 1883, L.V., c. 1883

ROYAL ROSE

Possibly Made by Thomas Dimmock

This deep dish is twelve sided and is panelled. The rim design is composed of three pairs of roses tied with flowing ribbons and three bold designs made up of twisting stems and tendrils that are serpentine in effect. Both designs extend almost to the center of the well where a medallion of roses and leaves is placed.

English,- impressed "Stoneware", looks like Mk. 1297, E.V., c. 1860

SAXONY

Maker Unknown

This sugar bowl is decorated with a design of stylized poppies very much like that on "Dresden" by Villeroy & Bach of Germany.

The lid is banded with a profile drawing of poppies and intertwined stems and buds. This pattern is also much like "Poppy" by Adams.

Probably German, marked N.S. & S., N.Y. (Import mark), Horseshoe mark like Thorn page 45, Mk. 43, probably L.V., c. 1900

SHANGHAI

Made by T. Rathbone & Co.

The scene on this plate with its oriental name is Swiss. A chalet is depicted at right, tall alpine peaks appear in the distance beyond a lake and tall elm trees at left are placed before village towers in the distance. A fence and flowers are in the foreground.

This scene appears on a baroque platter mold which is deeply scalloped and gilded. This picture might have been included in the Scenic category as it somewhat resembles Shanghai by Grindley.

English, marked T.R. & Co., like Mk. 3204, L.V., c. 1898

SHANNON

Made by Wedgwood

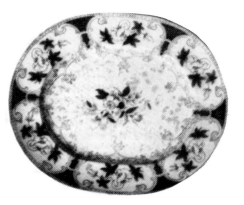

The flowers and vines on this platter are green but the leaves and dividing lines are printed in a very dark cobalt. The central flower is a green rose with cobalt leaves.

The shadow tracing of flowers in the background is in light green.

English, marked as above with the word "Pearl" impressed, M.V., c. 1855

SNOWFLOWER

Maker Unknown

Cobalt has been applied heavily to this vase and gold has been painted on the oriental fret-type handles.

The patterns appears to be a reversal of the usual flow blue process because the bluish white flowers are placed on the dark ground. Gold has been used to accent the details of the floral design.

Probably English or American, dated 1891, L.V., c. 1891

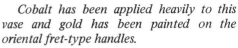

SUPERIOR

Made by Petrus Regout

This plate is almost identical to Waverly made by W. H. Grindley. The only difference is in the mold. The well is a bit deeper than in the English plate and the blue is not as intense. Otherwise the scalloping, beading, lacy embossing and pattern are the same.

Dutch, marked as above with a Sphinx mark, L.V., c. 1891

SYRIAN

Made by W. H. Grindley

The pattern on this basin is a concentric repetition of small squares placed to form a cross consisting of a dark blue center surrounded by a lighter blue tracing in a triangular form that fills in the corner.

On the pitcher that accompanies this basin the designs are all about the same size.

The central design consists of a medallion with the cross in its center surrounded by circles of triangular forms.

English, marked as above, Mk. 1842, L.V., c. 1891

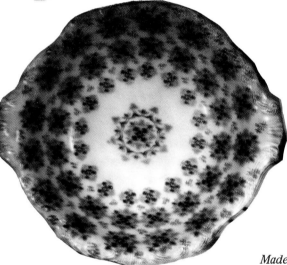

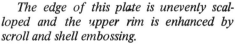

SYTON

Made by Till & Sons

The edge of this plate is unevenly scalloped and the upper rim is enhanced by scroll and shell embossing.

The design appears on the rim and consists of three rounded knobby forms, outlined with scrolls and enclosing small flowers and a lined diaper pattern. Sprays of flowers are placed beneath this and smaller similar designs are placed around the rim. An outer edging of the diaper pattern circumscribes the plate and appears at the top edge over the main design.

English, marked as above, Mk. 3858, L.V., c. 1891

TASAN
Made by Villeroy & Boch

Basket type dishes like this one were used for Hors d'oeuvres. The dish is divided into two sections and bears a center handle. On either side of the handle are small round recesses for condiments. A narrow brocade band is placed around the upper edge.

The vessel is covered with a design of oriental type flowers. A bird is perched among the blossoms at the right. Flowers are also printed around the outside of the body.

The correct title is Fasan (Pheasant). German, marked V&B, L.V., c. 1880

TOOTHBRUSH HOLDER
Maker Unknown

This small vase form is decorated with a triangular design of three large flowers set in a triangular basket form flanked by scrolls that are linked at the bottom by a garland of flowers. A pair of large scrolls extend from the top of the design. This toothbrush holder is part of a boudoir wash set.

Probably English, probably L.V., c. 1900

TRELLIS
Made by Ford & Sons

We show a set of pitchers that is typical of late Victorian design. Their tops are scalloped and heavily embossed, and so are the bases. A pansy is placed on the upper part of the body and beneath this is a rams horn design centered by a pendant from which swing swags of beads. The bottom part of the vessel is printed with stylized flowers placed on a trellis background.

English, marked F & Sons, Burslem, Mk. 1585, L.V., c. 1900

VENICE

Made by Pinder, Bourne, & Hope

The upper part of the rim of this gently scalloped plate is printed with a diaper design of quatrefoils set in diamonds. A floral pattern is placed below this. Three cartouches outlined with foliated cobalt and gold scrolls contain small coloured flowers of rose, orange, soft blue with green leaves. The cartouches are joined by a long scrolled curved cobalt and gold line which encloses a larger floral design of a burnt orange rose and a small pink flower. These are placed between gold and cobalt leaves. Small gold sprays are painted below the cartouches and enter the well. A single narrow gold circle appears in the center of the well.

English, marked P.B. & H., Mk. 3045, M.V., c. 1860

VENUS

Made by Thomas Till & Sons

The pattern on this covered vegetable dish is printed in slate blue. The design is composed of wreaths of foliated scrolls which are separated by stylized round bouquets of small flowers that are connected by swags of beads. Elongated leaves are embossed on either side of the handles and these are emphasized by gold lines.

English, marked as above, Mk. 3856, L.V., c. 1891

VINE

Made by Josiah Wedgwood

The outer edge of this plate is decorated with a narrow band of spear points and dots. The pattern name derives from the grape leaves and grapes and tendrils on the vine that wreaths the rim and the upper part of the well. Small flowers are twined about the stalk also.

The large flower in the center of the plate is a sunflower type.

English, marked impressed Wedgwood, marked impressed "Pearl", Mk. 4086. The plate is dated 1860, M.V., c. 1860

VINE

Made by Wedgwood & Company, Ltd.

This unevenly scalloped plate is gilt edged and is embossed with dainty scrolls and dots that are interposed with embossed designs of shells and pendant grapes. The design is asymmetrical and consists of a heavy grouping of large leaves and small flowers placed to one side of the rim and the well. From this, stems and leaves extend around the rim.

English, this Wedgwood & Company was formerly Podmore Walker & Company, Mk. 4059, L.V., c. 1906

WESTBOURNE

Made by S. Hancock & Sons

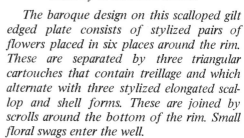

The baroque design on this scalloped gilt edged plate consists of stylized pairs of flowers placed in six places around the rim. These are separated by three triangular cartouches that contain treillage and which alternate with three stylized elongated scallop and shell forms. These are joined by scrolls around the bottom of the rim. Small floral swags enter the well.

The center medallion is composed of a central wreath containing the treillage pattern. This is enclosed by a circle of large and small flowers set within a spear point edge and finally by an outer wreath of stylized round flowers and pointed leaves which are joined by swags of flowerets.

English, marked S.H. & S., Mk. 1929, L.V., c. 1891

WINDSOR

Made by Ford & Son

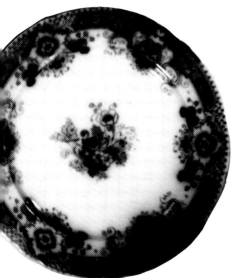

The rim of this plate is decorated with three large stylized two-toned flowers set against a diamond diaper pattern background.

These flowers are separated by a long scroll and triangular pendant design. The lower part of both designs enter the well.

The central bouquet consists of flowers and scrolls and a small vase form at left that contains two little posies.

English, marked F. & Son, Mk. 1587, L.V., c. 1893

YORK

Made by J. & G. Meakin

The butter pat photographed is scalloped. Three designs of floral wreath sprays and pendant flowers are joined by arched scrolls to three alternating designs of a small latticed oval cartouche with double leafy sprays beneath it.

English, marked as above, Mk. 2599, L.V., c. 1891

MISCELLANEOUS CATEGORY
PATTERNS WITH NO PICTURES AVAILABLE

BALMORAL

Made by Burgess & Campbell

This is the same pattern as "Royal Blue" listed in Williams, Book I, page 198 and as "Floral" by Hughes also listed in Williams, Book I, page 178 and "Senator", by J. Dimmock & Company listed in this book.

American, See Thorn, page 120, Mk. 33, L.V., c. 1880

HEUMANN

Made by John Maddock & Sons

The plates in this pattern are scalloped. The rim is printed with a long floral garland alternating with a shorter festoon.

In the center the two garlands are placed to form half a medallion with the longer one positioned under the shorter one.

English, marked as above, Mk. 246. L.V., c. 1891

EAGLE & SHIELD

This is the popular name for the pattern "Gem".

IVY

Made by Myott, Son & Company

This pattern has a scalloped edge and has floral and scroll embossing on the upper rim.

A design of small ivy leaves and tendrils surrounds the lower rim and the well defined by a narrow blue band.

English, marked as above, Mk. 281. L.V., c. 1900

MISCELLANEOUS CATEGORY
ADDENDA AND CORRECTIONS TO BOOK I

age 169 **"BEDFORT"**. *This is an hor d'oeuvre dish.*

age 169 **"BELLFLOWER"**. *This pattern was probably hand decorated with a stencil.*

age 172 **CAVENDISH"**. *We show a picture of a relish dish that displays the entire pattern.*

age 173 **"CONWAY"**. *This pattern is also found with the backstamp of Wood & Sons (Mk. 4285) who purchased the New Wharf Pottery in 1895. Some of the Wood & Sons blanks are scalloped, beaded, embossed and gilt edged.*

page 174 **"CYPRUS"**. *Made by Ridgway Bates & Company. We show another piece of thi ware. This is a small platter that shows a different center scene and a border tha contains small birds instead of butterflies that are placed in the rim design of bamboo fronds.*

page 180 **"GAINSBOROUGH"**. *We show a better picture of the pattern.*

page 181 **"HANNIBAL"**. *This pattern may not be Flow Blue, although the plate photographe is blurred.*

page 184 **"INDIANA"**. *This pattern may be borderline Flow Blue.*

page 186   **"KENWORTH"**. *We show a picture of the mold described. The scalloped plate was photographed in error.*

page 194   **"PAISLEY"**. *Last paragraph should read see Hartman, page 116.*

page 197   **RICHMOND"**. *This pattern may be borderline.*

page 198   **"ROYAL BLUE"**. *This pattern is also backstamped with the name "BALMORAL".*

page 199   **"SHELL"**. *This pattern also appears with a backstamp marked "W & C" – which represented "Wood & Challinor" who were working in c. 1840.*

"SPINACH". *This pattern was also made at Maastricht, Holland. The pattern should be categorized as brush-painted.*

page 205   **"VERONA"**. *This pattern was also made in cobalt blue and white, without the addition of the colours. We show a picture of this rendition.*

page 205   **"VINRANKA"**. *I have been informed by the importers, Swedish Products, Inc., Chicago, Ill., that production of this pattern was halted in April 23, 1967. Some stock was still available in 1968.*

page 207 **"FORTUNA"**. *We show a picture of a pitcher in this pattern. The collar is deeply scalloped and gold lustre has been placed around the edge. A thick band of flowers leaves and sprigs is placed around the top part of the vessel and this is contained by a row of embossed beading. The design on the body is composed of a central bouquet of small round fruits and flowers surmounted by an inverted triangular design of large leaves. Swags of bell flowers and scrolls flank the main design, and two of these extend vertically upward and terminate in triangular floral bouquets.*

English, marked as above, Mk. 2599, L.V., c. 1891.

page 208 **"MAPLE LEAF"**. *The examples found have not been Flow Blue. The cup and saucer shown carries a pattern that consists of large maple leaves set within a scroll reserve of treillage. Gold lines have been placed on the leaves. A smaller triangular design composed of fleur-de-lis alternates with the maple leaves and these designs are joined by garlands of bell flowers.*

So many dealers over the years have written about this pattern as Flow Blue that we will include it as it is impossible to state definitely one way or the other whether it comes in Flow Blue. But the reverse of the saucer in this set is faintly blue.

English, mark 2886, L.V., c. 1891

page 208 **"RUBUS"**. *We show a picture of the pattern.*

page 208 **"SEFTON"**. *We show a picture of this pattern.*

LAHORE

MADE
BY

P.S.

The above words mean that the writer has some material that she feels should be appended to the finished book: afterthoughts as it were.

The mark ⟨W⟩ was attributed to W&E Corn in Book I. This mark has now turned up with the word Germany under it. A letter elicited from Dr. Monika Homig-Sutter of the Keramic Institute in Munich states that she cannot locate such a mark in the reference books available to her. Mr. Karl Klein, of Harleysville, Penna., a well known authority in this country, writes that he feels that the attribution to W&E Corn is probably accurate and states that possibly Corn ordered hard china clay from Germany and had his mark put upon the pieces, but since they were decorated and fired in Germany they had to be so marked. I have found a saucer ("Quebec" listed in the miscellaneous part of this book) that is marked with the shield used by Utschneider in Germany and also marked with the ⟨W⟩ Perhaps Utschneider was making wares for the English potters.

RECENT DISCOVERIES

ATHENA
Made by W.H. Grindley
Shaving mug decorated with floral streamers. Mk. 1842. L.V., c. 1891

OSBORNE
Made by Ridgways
Egg cup. For pattern, see Book I page 124.

BIBLIOGRAPHY

POTTERY AND PORCELAIN 1700–1914, Bevis Hillier, 1968

THE CHINA TRADE, Carl Crossman, 1972

MASON'S PATENT IRONSTONE CHINA, Geoffrey A. Godden, 1971

THE DRAGON EMPRESS, Marina Warner, 1972

QUEEN VICTORIA, Pearl Woodham Smith, 1972

BLUE PRINTED EARTHENWARE, 1800–1850, Coyshe, 1972

THE BOOK OF POTTERY AND PORCELAIN, VOLUMES I and II, Warren Cox, 1970

THE DICTIONARY OF WORLD POTTERY AND PORCELAIN, Louise Ada Bolger, 1971

THE ENGLISH TABLE IN HISTORY AND LITERATURE, Charles Cooper

ENCYCLOPEDIA OF BRITISH POTTERY AND PORCELAIN MARKS, Geoffrey A. Godden, 1964

HANDBOOK OF POTTERY AND PORCELAIN MARKS, Cushion and Honey

HANDBOOK OF OLD POTTERY AND PORCELAIN MARKS, J. Jordan Thorne, 1947

PORCELAIN AND POTTERY MARKS, Hazel Hartman, 1943

CIVILIZATION OF GREECE IN THE BRONZE AGE, H. R. Hall, 1927

ANCIENT POTTERY OF THE HOLY LAND, Ruth Amiran, 1963

LIFE ON A MEDIAEVAL BARONY, William Davis, 1923

MARKS OF AMERICAN POTTERS, Edwin Barber, 1903

GLOSSARY

ACANTHUS A plant that grows in the Mediterranean region having toothed leaves. The stylized rendition of the leaves is used in architectural and classical design.

BUCOLIC Pastoral, rustic, countrified.

CASTELLATED Built like a castle with turrets and battlements.

CYMA CURVE A curve that is partially convex and partly concave.

FELDSPATHIC Containing feldspar, a mineral that occurs in crystals and which consists of silicate of alumina with soda, potash and lime. Potters clay is the material formed by the decomposition of feldspathic rock. It is a natural flux that promotes the fusing of pottery material in the kiln.

HUBRIS Excessive self confidence; to the Greeks, an arrogant insolence towards the Gods.

INDIGENOUS Born or produced naturally in a land or region.

ISLAMIC Pertaining to the Muslim faith based on the teachings of Muhammad, and the countries in which this is the dominant religion.

NEOCLASSIC Pertaining to a revival of styles from classical antiquity, particularly a severity of composition.

QUASI Resembling; seemingly but not really.

ROMANESQUE Pertaining to the style of architecture and ornamentation that prevailed in Europe from the close of the Classical period to the rise of Gothic design. The word "Romanesque" means "romantic" in French.

SCIMITAR SHAPED Curved, resembling an arc.

SERPENTINE Characteristic of a snake in form or movement.

STRIATED Furrowed, striped or streaked.

TUSCAN ARCHITECTURE Pertaining to one of the five classic orders developed in Rome, basically simple Doric style with little decoration.

VITRIFIED Converted into a glassy substance by exposure to heat, therefore "glass".

WINE CISTERN A vessel used for holding or storing wine.

INDEX

O – Oriental
S – Scenic

F – Floral
AN – Art Nouveau

M – Miscellaneous
B – Brush-Stroke Painted

* – Described or named in Book I

284

285

287

288

PRINTING
BY

Reynolds-Foley Co.
LOUISVILLE, KENTUCKY

BOB KELLOGG

COVER PHOTOGRAPHS